WASTING MY LIFE

James Miranda

Frontispiece

I had some help in pulling this book together, but 55% of it is my hard work, my proof that I know things, that I can read and write. So many so-called professionals in the teaching game have misjudged my abilities, simply going by a file. I knew I had to defend myself, to get back my opportunity to get an education and live. My father told me to be brave, that my good mind would work for me, and my integrity would carry me forward. So, helping me, he'd ask me questions, then I'd jot down notes. Then I'd tell him many things about my life, and he'd jot down notes. After many hours of questions and suggestions, the manuscript began to take shape. The three initial months soon became seven months of work, with so many rewrites and corrections. I have spoken my feelings about my life, and you will see that aside from the issue of 'competence', I do have a desire and a feeling for an academic life. I have reread the manuscript many times, every word of it. I wrote all my poems, and I even made typographical corrections in the computer, including grammar and spelling changes. It was my decision what to keep and what to throw out. I hope you like my book! And as Aristotle said:"We make war that we may live in peace."

James Miranda

WASTING MY LIFE

by James Miranda

AS TOLD TO:
R. Crowder, editor, enhancer,
auxiliary writer.

CHESTER HOUSE - PUBLISHERS
P.O. Box 1469, Grand Central Station
New York, New York 10163

This autobiographical writing is a true story; most names
have been made fictional, keeping the names of people I
love.

Copyright© 1993 by James Miranda

Jacket & Cover design: C. Hutchins

Library of Congress Catalog
Card No. 93-72729

Hardcover:ISBN 0-935763-02-3
Paper: ISBN 0-935763-03-1

Printed in the United States of America
Bookcrafters, Chelsea, Michigan
★★★★★★★★★★★★★★★★★★★★★★★★★★★★★★★★★★★★
Publisher
Chester House - Publishers
P.O. Box 1469, Grand Central Station
New York , New York 10163-1469
First edition - October 1993

Dedicated To:

First Lady Hillary Clinton, Ms. Marian Wright Edelman and the Children's Defense Fund, Atty. Lani Guinier; to all LD students who have suffered getting their schoolwork deemed 'satisfactory'; to Mom, to Grandma, to Dad No.1 (deceased), Dad No. 2 (who helped me so much with this book); to my four teachers: Miss Tibbs, Miss Nina Ross, Ms. Ardis Bourland, Mr. Alan Hubschman; to Dr. Weilin Wang, Dr. H. Chen, Dr. Ruth Howard, Dr. A. Kawachi; to the J. Gehms, the P. Hensleys, the L. Proctors; to Ms. Myrna Cheatham (my guardian), Virginia Butler, Pat Holly, Viola Holtzclaw, Linda Dattoma, Ed Dunham, and all the people who believe in me!

James Miranda

*****   *****   *****

"It seems I can hear God saying to America:
            YOU ARE TOO ARROGANT."

Rev. Dr. Martin Luther King, Jr.

INTRODUCTION

(Just as you sample a good wine before dinner, you may sample my book by reading this Introduction. J.M.)

Dear Reader, this book - all 132 pages of it - was read by me in draft status, more than one dozen times, with my job being to point out typographical errors, and this meant reading each line, each word. I was the only type-reader, so if you see any misspelled words, it's my fault! I certainly could not have carried out this work if I were "unable to read or write" as the mean LD woman at my first college said. And her suspicions of my abilities were quickly backed up by other teachers at WCC. As you know, when one graduates from high school with regular diploma and some honors, (as I did), and had a high near-ninety average, if you are classified as a " Learning Disabled student", (as I was) , in the first instance they are going to try to discourage you from the idea of going to college! In my case I was accepted at six colleges. We happened to pick Westchester Community College because it was nearest to my home. Now I think that was a grave mistake. It was not easy for me to get there. While it was a state-supported school, supposedly for the poor, practically every one there drove cars. I had to come there on a bus. I'd get up at 6:30 a.m., leave home at 7:30. to catch the one-an-hour bus. And the last bus to my town left the campus at five daily. I was excited about being in college, and having to do these things alone. My dad only helped me get familiarized the first week. He certainly helped me go through the maze of registration and selecting courses. But after that, I was on my own. The welcome by college officials was horrible! An LD student is treated precisely like a mentally-defected prisoner.

They have no faith at all in your ability: you are a marked person, treated much different than a so-called 'normal' student. You have to report to the LD office and they try to run your life, tell you what to do and when. The worst thing about this, they don't know you as a person and by what they say, they have a very low opinion of you. Most of us were minorities, and they did not treat you as they treat white students, LD or not LD. In your classes the teachers always sneer at you. In one particular class, I'd raise my hand during discussions and she'd never call on me! Any person going to school knows that your oral participation is very important. With Dad I had been many places around the world and had been with many important people. I had lots to share, but no opportunity! They failed

i

me in this class! Why? There is an attitude when you're classified as 'mentally defective'. And they can get away with any negative exaggeration of your performance! Listen, while just sixteen, I went all the way from New York to Flagstaff, Arizona and back, alone, changing planes in Chicago and Phoenix, and living for two weeks (with friends) , managing my eating and money alone. No, I am not mentally-retarded as these WCC teachers (reading my file) treated me. I listen daily to news broadcasts and I have my opinions about the money crisis, about floods, about crime, about movies. Yet, that basic skills teacher tried to avoid me rather than include me or let the class hear the many interesting things I could add to class discussions. In the end, she delighted in not passing me. That was cruel and very unfair of her. Just three days before the end of the semester Dad received a shocking letter from her department head, trying to outline my incapabilities, going back to the beginning of time (filewise). The one thing in the missive we could do something about, she said I didn't hand in three of seven assignments. (They all knew forgetfulness was a part of my malady.) Well, Dad made me sit down and spend six hours doing the missing lessons, then we rushed up to the campus and delivered them in person. But it was too late! She had already given me the bad grade before writing that letter. The letter was merely to cover her evil doings to me. She had no intention of passing me **(and that is supposed to be the idea of school).** There would be no thoughtful review of my performance. The negative prejudgment of me would suffice. Dad has saved the proof of my good work, which they knew deserved a passing grade.

Next, they had me taking a course called College Success, supposedly an easy survey course, and it was. I enjoyed every bit of it, and I knew all their topics very well. Even so, the teacher shocked me by giving me an F. Why? Politics and racism, and lots of thirst to do evil. This professor (they like to be called 'professor', and I'm courteous and a very proper student), first gave me A on two assignments, then, when the evil LD supervisor started knocking me, her opinion changed. She called my father accusing him of doing my papers, then gave me F. She didn't even know my father, **had never seen him,** but this is how prejudgment works!
The mystery here is: am I really such a bad egg, such a hopeless student, or is there something else working? The latter, you can bet! Daily I did my homework and I did it well. We had a

textbook by an Indian author and I knew that very well because it was about technical assistance to India. My father had been India officer at United Nations for more than a decade, and a specialist in technical assistance, and all these matters were often discussed at our dinner table, with foreign guests, often from India. So, why should I, James, have trouble with this easy course material I know so well? **Somebody's imagination of who I am and what I can do.** Yes, it was at mid-terms when the LD specialist, supposedly my mentor, got into the picture of running my life,and speaking only evil of me to my teachers. Why? **She had read my file.** She exaggerated saying *I could not read or write, and that I didn't belong there.* There was this desire to push down a minority LD student, and amazingly, ALL my teachers went along, eager to sack me! This writing is to say: I am very attentive to my schoolwork, always making progress. The system said there'd be a place for me. I come from an academic family. I am not a delinquent sitting around in college. I am not a lame-brain. Yet, you would **never** get them to admit their ganging up, plotting to fail me, was an act of gross racism. I believe this treatment rolled freely because they knew I'd been through the mills of foster care and adoption. My new father is (in their opinion) a **_Black_**, capable of *anything!* When the college success woman called him, accusing him of doing my paper, he explained calmly that I had worked very diligently on my paper for three or four weeks, and when I had ample time, I generally did very good work. Well, she didn't want to hear that. **They don't know me**, yet, they'd tear me down, and tear my father down. She possibly didn't know I had won two essay contests in high school, and $100, so the main issue here is:_*prejudgment*_. That something 'behind the scenes'. With the LD woman starting to arouse their suspicions about me just after mid-terms, there was this massive jumping on board, i.e., to *destroy* me. Alone, I remained confident of my academic skills, but it wasn't easy. I thought the idea of college was everybody being joyful, helping young people to learn. Such was not my experience at WCC. Nobody was in a helping or encouraging mood; it was all a **war** with them trying their best to push me down, to smother me.

Before the fall term, Dad and I had visited the campus several times in the summer of 1992, and had had meetings with members of the staff. The LD woman, then, didn't have any time for

iii

us (she was supposedly away on another assignment). Then the minute school began, and I reported to her office, she again was away and I was assigned to her assistant. The assistant woman was very nice in the beginning. Lo and behold, at mid-terms , here came the main LD woman into the arena, ready *to judge me*; well, the nice assistant lady changed colors. The LD boss charged at me like a tiger, saying I hadn't been at the special skills lab, and nobody had told me it was compulsory. With my tight schedule of classes (half of which were remedial, i.e., you pay tuition on them but you get no credit), and with the one-bus-an-hour to my town, it was impossible for me now to go to so many extra labs to improve my reading or writing when I was improving it nicely in my daily work at home. As an LD student, I was supposed to get extra time on final exams, and be tested in isolation, but this *never happened.* Because, the LD woman created trouble for me in every way she could. The real issue, she did not like my father, and after one meeting banned him from campus. Of course, her behavior was racist, very racist, but she kept trying to point out my weaknesses as the cause of trouble. So, they struck me out, supposedly by my poor performance. Supposedly.

Actually, what the LD student faces, they read your file, and whatever is in that file, that's your life, you cannot escape it. They grind you down from that position; they do not make an effort to build you up. You are something inferior! I believe most LD students face a bit of this terrible prejudice. I had in my baggage a few more things they did not like. And there seems to be no laws, no back-up supervision to dissuade them from their folly of bringing us **down**. (That is, those of us they assume are from the underclass, or big-city ghetto.) They regard themselves as teaching giants, with neither empathy nor mercy. In appearances, it was such a beautiful campus, such a beautiful beginning for me, going each morning at 7:30 to this beautiful new life at Westchester Community College. But at the outset the LD woman said I did not belong there! recommending that I plan to stay 'nine or ten years' for a basic two-year degree! Just imagine, why would anyone want to keep a student nine or ten years on a two-year campus? Am I that stupid? No. It's a prejudgment, plain and simple. Imagine such appraisals put before my teachers causing them to have second thoughts about me, negatively. Finally, a consensus for a criminal was devised: they gave me all F

iv

grades, and R for Repeat. I can't imagine this happening to a good, middle-class white student who comes to school every day, prepared and agreeable. A kid from a good home, a place of culture. In my case, it was imagined that I'm something less, deserving less. ***And, they could get away with it!***, That's the main reason for this book. They could get away with it! And of course the idea of it was to teach me (and my father) our place. Theirs was the *power* to say I didn't belong there, and the power to make it look like I didn't belong there. So, I had to say good-bye to my exhilarating new routine of study, to my few friends there. Lose all that time and credit, and seek a new beginning at another college.

Next I came to Queensboro Community College, and again, I was very much at home. However, at the outset one official lady there read my file and said I didn't belong there! *Where do I belong?* And so, the negative days began anew, just when most 'normal' students were getting settled down. I took the stress of it and did my best. And what followed, three equally negative and impatient teachers decided to give me the lowest grades (in spite of many good evidences of my being able to do good work). But I was a **marked** man, an LD student, and I was slower in my work than other students. While Dad and I thought they were , by law, to let me do my work at a slightly slower pace, they had no patience with that law. Many but not all were out to punish me, to show me that I didn't belong. *It was not an atmosphere for learning.* There was no help, no encouragement, no considering properly my weakened position as against the freedoms a normal student would have. For LD students there is often a fabricated stage of unworthiness. Yes, that new college I went to in the New York area was precisely negative like the first one when it came to a proper environment for an LD student. The reason: teachers were over-proud, non-helping, and not supervised enough in their handing out of evil grades, undeserved.

I have loved music since my pre-school days. My dying father gave me a flute which I cherish before I had reached my teen years, and I still have it. I've studied guitar privately for five years, and I play my guitar every day. The many melodies I know seem to soothe me nicely, and sometimes I take my guitar out, and play for others. I did it in high school, and at parties. Now I'm living with my adoptive father who is a great organist and violist, having played under some of the most celebrated conductors in the world. But he is not a white man. A so-called black man, others would judge. Nevertheless, he is great and has inspired me immensely. Under him I've studied violin, piano and music theory. This is only my second year of piano exposure but I am making steady progress, and I like it.

So, when I enrolled in QCC I purposely took courses which I thought would be easy for me, Spanish and two music courses, plus the high school stuff they demand of you called 'Basic Skills'. Upon entering college the diplomas earned by LD students practically mean nothing as they see to it that you do not get into any normal science or social science courses until they, these new people, are satisfied with your ability to read and write! Ladies and gentlemen, this judging of elementary ability is very flawed with great misjudgments and prejudice. And as there are no checks and balances in the system, one or another mean teacher can get away with any dirt they want to practice through the grading system. As for my Spanish class, my teacher was not a bad sort. I liked her. But as I was a bit slower than the normal first-year student, she had her doubts about my ability to keep up, or to pass. It was forgotten that I could understand orally most any Spanish spoken. Yes, I was having difficulty with verbs and grammar, but I was working at it, and I could have succeeded, in time. But she asked my father to withdraw me, and he did. Now some say there should have been a definite slot for me, a slow learner, but teachers can be impatient and expect us to keep up with their fastest students. And, the system does not allow them to "carry me" without penalty in grading.

Now, the two music teachers I had were something else! I was taking beginning piano and a course called Introduction to Music which was mostly a drilling on key signatures and chords, which I had been learning quite well at home and with my private guitar teacher. Credit for the courses was to be based on attendance, performance, and our going to two concerts and writing about them. For the latter assignment I wrote first about an organ concert my dad gave in Bronxville. I first asked the teacher would this be okay. With somewhat of a sneer and raised eyebrows, he said 'okay'. Next, I brought my father to the school auditorium to attend an orchestra concert whereby both my music teachers would be performing, one as conductor and the other as viola soloist. Dad and I both enjoyed the concert which he said was excellent. We went backstage so he could meet my two teachers. Later he wrote them a letter of congratulations, and made it known that he himself had studied viola under Ralph Hirsch (in a scholarship) and under Thor Johnson, conductor of the Cincinnati Symphony, who in turn was a student of famed Emanuel Vardi. He is equally beautifully trained in organ having studied with Dr. Palmer Christian at the University of Michigan, Claire Cocci, Jesse Crawford, Mario Salvatore at Santa Croce in Florence, Italy, and Claudia Dumschat now at St. Paul's, Columbia University. I am almost certain Dad's fine background in music did not sit well with my teachers. They decided to teach me and Dad a lesson. They both gave me F in the course, and the College immediately put me on probation! This injustice made me very ill, and Dad began immediately seeking redress, but under the system, no redress exists. A teacher can mar your life like this, without ever having to prove precisely how you are "a failure". The loophole is the LD tag, as **all** of us are suspected of being grossly stupid. And in the system, it is assumed that **all** teachers are honorable, and that their grading of students is without flaw or favoritism. Of course it is a matter of judgment, and a thousand things can go into judgment. What I am saying is that with all the racism very active in present-day America, the system needs a *rare* thing: **teaching with NO racial bias.** Certainly racist teachers are plentiful, holding back particularly Blacks and Hispanics. Yes, I've met **too many** who delight in <u>killing you</u> like this. Without justification.

And now, I have no credit for my one year of steady hard work where I certainly made progress, and was progressing as well as some so-called 'normal' students. Just a bit slower, that's all. They've left me with nothing for my tuition money. Absolutely nothing. Is it the end of life? Almost. But I wonder if they ever thought of my future and what I am trying to do? No. All they want to say is: **_You Don't Belong Here._** Then, where do I belong??

Dad says he **never** heard of any student getting an F in music, not in his 55 years in music. Maybe there is *something else* to it other than my ability or performance. In the first instance, I can tell you, Learning Disabled students often suffer greatly under teachers who assume they are stupid and not normal, and make no efforts to encourage you to *higher levels.* They love to pick at your

vii

assignments, look for flaws, and regard you as "mentally retarded". And most of us are **not** that. Also the official LD tab, that classification, makes people freely fail you (and administrators go along, never questioning what the teacher has done with you or to you) . They get by scot free, behaving as if you are a criminal or prisoner. Some will never treat you humanly; no encouragement. Very few will help you move upward in life. The idea seems to be: to punish, to hold back, to stigmatize.

I hope I can tell this story in an interesting manner, because the handling of LD students really needs correction. And, who is to say we don't belong in college when we have successfully graduated from high school? My purpose was to become a teacher of the Learning Disabled, but it can never happen if I have to go through the double scrutiny of over-proud racist teachers who know they can say anything about LD kids, and **get away with it**. Really, it should be the concern of all Americans. What I have experienced has definitely been an injustice, and if we are going to get to the bottom of the flaws in the present-day American Education System, we have to look not so much at delinquent or wayward students, but at delinquent and wayward teachers. Yes, in my case where I worked very hard at my studies, and I learned a great deal, there was that "something else" that made them count me out with undeserved F grades, the lowest they could give, to make me remember that I am inferior. At the same time, newly-arriving Chinese students in my classes got As and certainly they were not better in comprehension or expression than I was, with or without my disability. I would have been satisfied with a C, but the whole thought of it makes me shout: Americans need to do away with this awful grading system! And consider too, in the teacher's mind he has an idea of where that Chinese boy will fit in the future as a contributing citizen, and where they think I will fit in. A whole year of my life, **wasted** with half-crazy college people, prancing with too much power. Ungraciously they've spoiled my record so that I can do nothing in life. An academic life, which has always been my calling, no matter what they say!

James Miranda

London, England
June 14,1993

****** ******

WASTING MY LIFE

CHAPTER ONE

In medieval times you might have heard of a story that ended: "They killed my son because of my good fortunes," or, "They killed my son once they had enough bread and wine." While we're eight hundred years from those barbaric times, the thirst to destroy is still an active part of the life of man. With all our gadgets and material progress, we behave to each other in barbaric ways. The world of men hasn't changed much.

Why would one man want to waste his strength maligning another man? Well, they tell me the answer is Fear. And also Greed. They group off to protect privileges over others, and this behavior has kept us a part of the animal world. The Vile world, when we have attributes to be better than beastly animals. As the human world gets more heavily populated, and diverse groups are closer together, dishonesty in cross-relationships seems to thrive. While nice, God-fearing people can go places and find other like-people who live together very well, this is not the atmosphere of New York City, my home, and once America's greatest city. Utopia then is people living happily together, with compassion (this is a new word for me; I found it after talking a long time to my father about this problem). Compassion. It is still difficult for me to remember the meaning of such words for a long time. Maybe because I do not use them every day. I do know this word `power'. It goes back to the days of kings and their soldiers. And it is among us today, with all those people who have good jobs, including teachers, there is a thirst to use power unjustly in dealing with us smaller people.

Whereas power had been among kings and their soldiers for a long time, as the world has progressed, it is now mostly among

2

large ruling groups who should be identified as `ordinary' but who really think of themselves as `separate' and `special'. They help their friends and brothers into positions of power (over the rest of us). Whereas I did not start this book to discuss racism, it is certainly a power problem, and clearly lasting in most American cities today. The institutions are filthy with injustices.The old family life meant working, eating, and respecting each other. And education was a tool in it. A getting-readiness. Not so today. It is a profession for some to abuse others! Of course, we need education, some skills, but there are those in the game who do not want everybody to have the education or the skills , and they work viciously to keep some of us out. I AM ONE OF THOSE SO ABUSED!

In 1904 our government banned dancing among Indians because the white man feared some evil force or power would come in allowing Indians to practice their dance ceremonies. Well, the white man's fear put undue pressure on Indians for some years, then in the 1930s, the ban was lifted. The white man had conquered his fear, or, he had learned with a little compassion that Indians are harmless, and Americans too. Ladies and gentlemen, my main topic is education and how a similar fear has created an atmosphere of exclusion and denial, not to educate some of us. While teachers want us thinking altruistically of their roles, many have misused their positions to venomously hold back some of us, then lie, and declare that we, the students, have not done our jobs. And American society while catering to its underlying fears of racial sub-groups, denies that we are maligned and mistreated in the school setup. This terrible imbalance in education is being created viciously, and must be stopped! While statistics tooted are gloatingly pro-white, they don't show the deliberate dishonesty of teachers making the ability of nonwhites less than it is. Of course, most black and Puerto Rican students are behind most whites in aptitudes and cultural knowledge, but just consider how many bright ones from the Ghetto are deliberately punished with low grades by biased white teachers, especially at the college level!

Nobody gives the truth of how we are treated in the classroom, and how the system allows this dishonesty to continue. In this main matter of treatment, my other group, the Learning Disabled, should not be so behind the norms, or so powerless if the care, reporting and grading, were more honest in the education setup. I'm wanting government officials , the influential at the top, to see from my story the undue power of evil teachers (who want minority and LD students to lose out), and how they will dedicate themselves to downward pushing rather than lifting up and inspiring young students. We can't keep paying high teaching salaries for such treatment! Some say we need new laws and better enforcement of old laws, to ensure that everyone equally gets his share of quality education, but my emphasis is: to go forward in education, outside the question of financing, to improve American education on the whole, we need to recognize :*butchery*, the very evident racial injustice on the part of teachers, and take away the power they have to do harm through dishonest grading.

While dramatizing the pitfalls facing minorities, I also want to emphasize unmet needs of my other group, the `Learning Disabled'. Yes, they've put a tab on us which works in the same fashion as racism. Believe me when I tell you, too little is being done to recognize that the mere labeling alone unleashes a world of powerful abuses in our education, made so negative as <u>not</u> to inspire us to higher goals. Just look at the concentration which hallows the idea that LDs are only fit for blue-collar work! Yes, it is the ATTITUDE of the teaching world, so negative when it is supposed to be there to help us get up, not to an inferior level but to the <u>same</u> level as other studying people! Little-supervised teachers have poor vision of our capabilities; and the way they educate us, they place us: *Lowly in the World.*

This book is mainly about me, a sensitive academic person , minority and LD, who has had to strive very hard to get an education where vicious teachers and administrators have tried to hold me back. They lie about your preparation and your performance. Their negative way is not unlike that of people running foster care and adoption centers: they really don't want to see the children adopted as it takes from THEIR JOBS! And, for teachers to give LD students credit for having good minds and ability to thrive as well as normal students, is asking too much. They want to *criticize* us, mainly. **Make us feel badly about ourselves.** This may be all right as a theoretical approach, but when it becomes the accepted treatment in America, it is wrong. Also there's too much concentration on the *written record* about LD kids. It kills us as much as a gun in a murderer's hand.

Our so-called free system of education is not free; paradoxically, my schooling was a prison, with those to teach me being the jailers.

4

You'll see from my details how the flaw of judgment and grading grows and grows in our educational system, hurting LD kids and minorities, and I implore you to do something about it. These wicked people, educators and administrators, have chosen unconsciously or unfairly to _separate us_ from so-called normal white students, to downgrade us, to harm us and hold us back. The system allows it! and for us there is no redress.

I have had to write this book as such dishonesty has put me at a deadend in my young life, when I want to move ahead, and my mind and capability are ready to move ahead. No, the decision to destroy my life was made by well-paid teachers in public institutions, and co-signed by their equally over-titled administrators. Yes, uncaring teachers, paid by my father, have tried to crush my life. Now, you , the society, _Make Them Care!_ for people like me. Make them accountable! I've told you the problem which is killing me, and others like me. It was my wish that teachers would earnestly do their job and give me my grades and the best education possible, but they do not even come close to this fairness. They are OBSTRUCTIONISTS, ready to create a bad record from which we can never escape! Society, perhaps you do believe they represent me, that they're doing an honest job, that I am possibly the impossible one! No, a thousand times no! Just for once, please look on the other side. For years I have loved school; I go to school daily; I do my work, yet I must live with any dishonest teacher that comes upon the scene; obey her, be her fool, to get a grade. Nobody looks at her dishonest notices of my performance (always lower than actual because of her idea of my inferiority). EVERYTHING IS MY FAULT. Where they've not had the interest in helping me, I'm still the problem while they are the paid professional!

Misreading who I really am is part of the game. In the chair and thinking lowly of us, they have the license to say bad things about us. If you come from a good, cultured family, one as good as theirs, they often resent this, (as they think of you **first** as an underclass or minority, as something beneath them!), and they will mark you down, to bring you back DOWN to your place! They seldom let you escape upward in life. It is as if they have been chosen to be the keepers of the keys. For an LD kid or minority to grow higher in the world, they have to give sanction. They know this, and they abuse your rights and your good efforts. Mainly, they do not think of you as one **they** want to go up in the world!

5

White teachers don't respect you, they don't respect where you come from, and they don't listen to you. They run the show **with their prejudices intact**. I've seen them helping themselves to praise, fat paychecks , with clear consciences, while daily making me SQUIRM. (I had to look up the spelling of this word. It seems unAmerican, but I'll accept it not knowing from whence it came.) If you call me bitter at the outset, just remember, the evil has existed, uncorrected. I've been scarred by such injustice continuously from my first days at school, and the arrogance grows and gets crazy at the college level in America. Bold, ugly arrogance! I've tried to help myself away from it, but teachers are **the writers of the record**. They can do all sorts of unfair DAMAGE to me. Many of us so scarred often walk away , or, drift away defeated, and unprepared to get good jobs. <u>Yet, we know we have good minds!</u> I've refused to accept such bias against me, and look for good men to see these flaws in the academic world! I want them to see the evil of CATEGORIZING. It is to be challenged, and done away with. Otherwise, so many good lives (as mine) will be ruined.

I don't know exactly why but big city teachers today, wearing that negative chip, are more apt to judge you first, by what group you belong in, then teach you accordingly. This is prejudice! What I've experienced was: low appraisal of who I am, then, control, control, control. I saw among them very little love of teaching ; no empathy or love of me; but an urge to get two messages across: (a) they are in the driver's seat, (b) I am inferior to them. For me school has been years of magnifying my God-given weaknesses and constant biting attacks. And they have no patience at all for a slow learner. It seems from television that big American cities all have problems getting the 'underclass' educated. The talks seldom blame the teachers.   They blame our homes or the budget. They talk as if we need downward changes in the curricula, or special government programs. The system needs to concentrate on: students' needs. Or, fair appraisal of students' needs. People in public schooling need to become listeners. There are enough funds, but NOBODY IS LISTENING TO THE STUDENT. Teachers don't encourage or reward individual progress, but elate themselves in failure-giving. And they are not at all flexible: "Do it my way or I'll give you failure!" **(This is a demented frame of mind.)** American teaching suffers such behavior and attitudes. If things were okay with this method, then why should America be so behind Germany and Japan? This relates to why so many of us in the underclass are pushed out of school, and headed towards crime and nothing good in life! I speak out for so many who have the deep yearning to get educated, and we have obeyed the rules and done school work at our best, yet, the teacher denies us the reward of passing, of getting an education. In the profiling, people like me are lumped with delinquent kids, as if we're **all the same!** And, it matters what these people in authority think of us! So, I say, please, DON'T LUMP US WITH TRASH! We deserve something more of life.

Teachers largely control what happens in ghettoes by treatment, i.e., whether or not they are nice or fair to young students who need help. The tendency is to concentrate on the profile, to grade the profile or how you hate the profile; the individual is made to suffer, and he is completely forgotten as **someone who has rights,** yearnings, and entitlement. I've worked hard under many teachers who want to control my life with false ideas of who I am. And when they grade you, that one year, they do so, not only for the one year you may be in their classes *But for Your Entire Life. . .By What They Do To You That One Year.* And, ladies and gentlemen, that controlling they do snuffs out many hopes and fires of desired careers. Quite logical careers which could have been achieved by a so-called minority child, with proper support. Teachers should be asked constantly: HAVE YOU SERVED EACH AND EVERY CHILD WITH GOOD PURPOSES?

I was always studious, and I tried to be as good as the next student in all my studies. I learned a very great deal but learning is not enough. In the American system the grading has been made more important than the learning. I faced people who would control you like a jail warden controls prisoners. But their judgment of your worth is the more important thing. Those of us who deeply want an education, want to be judged fairly, but too often in modern America we do not get that. And this hurts the future of the whole country. So, my story could easily begin:"Through me they tried to kill my father because he urged them to let me be a free colorless soul ready to get my promised education." He had hoped they'd see me above my several misfortunes and do a good teaching job with what's good of me, and for which my dad has paid his high taxes. Instead , my misfortunes whetted their appetites; they saw an opportunity and they jumped at it, to kill me, TO SHOW ME MY PLACE. And by all means, they wanted to put my father in his place. They had the power to do this, and he was the culprit for putting grandiose ideas

7

into my head. When I finally got to college, I was so happy in my first days. While accepted at six schools, I decided on two very close to my home. This was a mistake. I would go through a whole year of steady, conscientious work, only to receive their arrogant sneers, and their lowest grade, an F.

Early in grammar school I accepted the label Learning Disabled when I first heard it applied to me. Yet, I knew that I was as smart as most people in many ways. I guess my efforts were to prove this to the teachers. But, usually they had already made up their minds and all my hard work meant absolutely nothing. I felt hurt when teachers began singling me out and giving me less than the normal students. Yes, teachers handle Learning Disabled kids in a certain negative way. And mostly, we accept it. **We're not to have any fancy ideas about our futures.** And, the so-called Learning Disabled specialists are not better than the others! They have their IEP meetings and Guidebooks and most of their handling of us is terrible. Here, society, I address you to consider the specialist's preparation and whether enough time was spent on examining himself or herself as to how they would treat others, the weak others who may come to the world in weaker physical circumstances or environments. I've seen among such so-called specialists much false pride , so much superior feeling.

Yes, they think themselves superior to me when they label me, and dictate the path of my life. They all know I came from a broken home, with physical damages at birth, with years in foster care, and finally with a good foster father who loves me, wants me to achieve, without malice. However, this new man who adopted me is not white (teachers know this) and he is richer and more cultured than most of my teachers (they know this too!). Whereas one would think my new life should be one of promise, my teachers have viciously tried to hold me back, and keep me down, and point out to my new father that THE BOTTOM is where I belong! This might be okay for a bad child, one who is lazy , uninterested in school or disrespectful, but I am none of those things, _Still_, they've spitefully taken delight in holding me down.

Listening to the problems I've had to face at school, my new dad first tried to stand middle ground, telling me that I must make special effort to obey teachers, that all teachers demand respect and that we should think of them as our superiors. We are to listen to

8

them as we listen to our parents. Well, my parents have always said good things about me. They have hugged me and they have helped me along. I've never gotten that from school teachers in New York. Never!

Teachers certainly profit in a system that lets them shine as independent superiors. They have the authority, the high salaries, the control over your daily life, for years and years. Yet, very few have ever talked to me as a human being. Recently on television I've heard reports of school districts trying new things: Oregon, Rochester and Kentucky. Former Governor Kean of New Jersey reported on a Kentucky scheme that brings parents right into the picture of their child's education. Well, my new father watched me work very hard at my homework. He saw where teachers misgraded me, downward. He was flabbergasted, and he changed his opinion about my attention to school work. He saw where I needed support, not criticism. He felt the low grades were unjust. He became a strong fighter for improvements at their end. He joined a parent group and he visited the school whenever they wanted him. But, he too faced great arrogance! They were ready to discount his great brains, his superior schooling. They wanted to push him down. And they wouldn't even listen to him to find out what my life has been. All they considered, they could consult their stupid record file on me, and go on with hardness from there. They made all the decisions, and the lies about my performance continued and grew. And on the question of my future they'd pick something very lowly and degrading for me. After middle school I became completely tired from trying so hard, and I knew I could never please them. For years I had tried to do everything they asked for the sake of good relations, a grade, and my parents. My new father made me realize that I am somebody too! I had to fight them to stay whole. I was too shy, he said, too accepting. He asked me to tell him everything that happened at school, and when I began telling him, he dropped many important things in his life, to help me. When you criticize modern schools, he learned, you get a lot of sass and a lot of paper in return. The authorities make sure new problems arise. Seeing so much mistreatment he knew he had to continue to fight, for me. Somewhere he thought he would meet a higher authority who would realize: the system needed policing, and it wasn't happening.

Now, that I have high school away, and am finding the same nonsensical prejudice in college, I am beginning to rebel against an educational system which I think has become rotten in America, by tolerating ugly dishonesty on the part of teachers, aiming at just the opposite of what they're put there to do. People don't complain enough! Maybe because bad treatment doesn't necessarily happen to white children. Yet, the Learning Disability mistreatment certainly affects white children. I want everybody to know, the system acts to HURT CERTAIN CHILDREN. Teachers with their titles and their wealth have to be supervised more, put under control so that those of us who have disabilities can develop in spite of our disabilities, and not become a burden on society. Among the teaching world, I think, theirs is too much privilege in controlling our lives, without proper respect for us. Review their tactics! Their superior attitudes are out of control and need to be checked!

When we were small kids there was a joke; we were asked if you could rub your stomach and pat your head at the same time. Or say:'Peter Piper picked a peck of pickles.' Many teachers want much more from the learning disabled. Much more. They need to relax and come down to earth and see what harms they are doing, standing back, criticizing, and not helping enough. Most are TOO IMPATIENT to help the learning disabled properly. Teachers must be forced to make something of us, and not tear us down.

Years ago a person followed a profession with a yearning to serve, and you'd train to serve. Today, it's to 'dictate' to some helpless people under you. Some, in first order think of themselves as scholars, professors and executives. Some even call themselves `underpaid middle-class' and `abused' by such balancing things as Affirmative Action. They've labeled me `Minority' and `Retarded' and seldom gave me as much as one inch of room to catch up and thrive as other students thrive. In fact, most of them were greatly disturbed by my 'slowness'. Too often they were ready to punish me for being 'slow'; and the vicious ones would fail me outright if I so much as forgot to hand in one of ten lessons. The nine good ones did not matter! Failure was what they wanted for me! And nobody thought about the many hours I worked at home, preparing my lessons. Good lessons, my father said they were. Those teachers controlling me never looked at my steady progress but always they'd harp on my being last in the class at several things (Not All!). My thirst to learn, my privilege to learn was never in their minds. After feeling their knifing me so many times, I muffled my screams and my tears. I wanted to let the world know that my mind was as good as theirs, and in this, I found myself putting down my thoughts, and maybe by doing so I could help others who are more needy than myself.

I was a strange mixture for them: a ghetto child, a minority, a rather homeless child, adopted, no real family YET, on the other side, NOW, I was well-to-do, living in a wealthy suburb; and my new family were educated nonwhite people (having more degrees than my teachers)! Teachers taking all this in, determined to punish me rather than to help me. The easy outlet was the fact that I was learning disabled! They could give me anything low, and I should have to accept it. But why? I guess this is part of a flaw in the American way of life. They wanted to **Show Me My Place**, and , ladies and gentlemen, this kind of racism is present in our school system, dancingly free to smash my life. Teachers and administrators do not see me as a colorless American, ready to make a contribution to my country. _My Contribution._ They tell me I have _Nothing_ to offer!!

In a so-called Basic Skills class I've seen them give new-arriving foreign kids (Indians, Chinese), who can barely speak the language, A while I get F. And my speaking is just as good as the Chinese boy's. Why? _Teachers Are the Keepers of the Keys_ to the riches of the world; they have an idea where the Chinese boy can go in the world. That same 'idea' does not apply to me. They have labeled me, and they do not think that I am in a category whereby the riches of the world should come to me. In fact, many think the country's riches, such as an education, would be wasted on me!! The system allows so-inclined teachers to floor me with such prejudice and mean predictions, and, I can do absolutely nothing about it.

It's a sick feeling when teachers fail you when you've made the extreme effort and have done your best and prepared yourself. And the test paper of failure is a Secret you never see. All through the long beautiful semester you've seen yourself as equal to others in the class. With more than fifty percent of white Americans thinking nonwhite Spanish and Blacks as much _lower_ than everybody else (whether or not they would admit it or see this as racism), it is there in this glorious majority opinion that some teachers **Relish in the Easy Path of Judgment**, and of giving me (and my kind) the lowest grade! Some do this viciously, others do it unconsciously. Nevertheless it hurts me unfairly. It hurts my family. It hurts

11

America. A few who think of themselves as conscientious and honest did it nonchalantly in collusion with one or another teacher, and both thinking grades for me didn't matter, that I would somehow survive owing to my second father's good provisions, being better than what most minorities get. Well, that's none of their business; I am an individual , to be free of their conclusions of where I belong in life. The law should not allow their suppositions to tie me down. The law should make them recognize and honor *My Efforts, My Progress*, and give me a **fair** grade I have earned. And if a nasty one can get by putting me in a pit of the lowest denomination, without having to prove it to anybody, i.e., my so-called failure, then something is grossly wrong in the system. I believe there should be some overseer to make such a teacher behave! They in a way are children too! Make them show every detail of my failure, or, in the end, pay for it!

When teachers want more pay (I've heard that Sandra Feldman woman on radio) they talk as if they've done everything good for their students; I never got an ounce of encouragement from them. Never! I was a write-off failure, to them. Nobody tried to build up my **self esteem**; in fact, the school system has hurt my self esteem more than anything else. (I think teachers reading this will sigh in disgust still looking for a way to blame me.) Furthermore, it is said many teen suicides are due more from teacher-mistreatment than home-mistreatment. I wonder if the fact that so many teachers are themselves new in middle class accounts for the way they abuse us. And among these biased bigwigs, there are a lot of new Americans, not really knowing the American way. They should know that some nonwhite families are just as good as theirs, in every way! They should be urged to come out of their hoity-toity cloud, **down**, to do a real teaching job. The system should make them give me **something positive** for my time, efforts, and money. All they seem to want is to *Boss*, and to get: MORE OF THE PIE!

Greed of course is a part of my subject, but let's start with the spread of wealth through the rigid (and biased) selecting of *who is qualified* to move ahead (they start right in at the basic school levels). Right away: you're a category, to be pampered or despised. The dropouts really don't want to drop out. I know. They tried to make me a dropout, but I resisted it with all my strength. And I won in this battle! I gradually saw through all that hypocrisy and greed: all those phony titles, just for themselves. . . so-called servicing the public, the needy, and deciding who is qualified to join their privileged group of being recognized as educated. And the insensitivity to those of us who do not have the speed to keep up with Joe or Sue. (My teeth and tongue get mixed up on this word: 'insensitivity' , but with practice, I am getting better at it.) And wagging a finger they'd say: "You don't belong here.""You won't get a job." "You have no business in office skills or college prep." "You'd never be an artist, or a musician, or a teacher!""You won't get high skill or any titles."   What in the hell, White Teacher and White Society, am I supposed to be in life, huh?? All your **devilment** and discrediting of me is an evil you cannot get away with. Those transcripts where you've put F for me, seem more indelible in this computer age. . .they'll give me a <u>NO</u> in many places where I go for more schooling or a job, but in the end, I won't blow away, and I won't let you profile me out of existence that way!

*****   *****   *****

CHAPTER TWO

Now, in the suburban schools, in the very good neighborhoods where I had the occasion to attend, strangely they were always saying:"You don't belong here!". I knew it was not a fair judgment of my work, my brain, or my ability. Again it was plain old American racism! Dressed up to look like professional talk. Would I let this ruin my life? Dad and I decided: NO!! Quietly we began fighting. The very first of it was hours and hours of review, and work with four private tutors, and very little time for pleasure for me. Few friends, few trips out of the house. . . yet, the teachers continued sending home notes that said I was not studying, not doing my homework, and they'd telephone my dad constantly if I forgot so much as a pencil. He calmly tried to remind them that forgetfulness was part of my malady, but they would not listen at all. Failure was what they wanted for me, and I was always judged against the best and not against my peers. And where, ladies and gentlemen , do I really belong? Those teachers who would deny any suggestion of racial bias had never thought of me beyond that delightful moment of giving me a failure grade. It annoyed them that my adoptive father asked to see results, and when he challenged the results, they were livid with anger. If I did all my math problems correctly and merely left out a decimal point, they'd mark it zero and I'd get no credit for my four months of hard work. It happened time and again. They were not concerned about MY NEED TO MOVE UPWARD. Dad and I won a few battles, otherwise, I would have never finished high school. It was a rare teacher who was really concerned about my future. . . yet every teacher even the not-so-bad ones was in the picture all the time, writing down negative stuff on me, creating a permanent record I could not escape. I thought all teachers should be thinking of our futures. I was wrong.

Learning Disabled children are all profiles. If there is something previously thought-out about us, it usually is negative. We belong where the worst in our records tells them we belong. No need to try new things with us! In the several special education classes I attended teachers did not take the time to explain things. There were tons of notebook exercises to do, and they'd get corrected.

14

That's all. All the real explaining for me to understand things was done at home. Most of the LD children in my classes were saddened because the teachers had no positive feelings about them. They were merely 'keeping house'. And, we all heard the nasty things they'd say behind our backs. From my earliest years I was always eager for school but the bad treatment of teachers grew more and more unbearable and I really felt like others in the class: _Why Don't I Just Stay Home?_ Of course our parents encourage us in a positive way to go to school every day and to make the best of it. What's in our future when we quit and merely hang in the streets is usually a going downward with the wrong people. But we are going downward in school, with the wrong teachers! And their wrong judgment of our progress. School should not be a prison; for LD children, it often is.

So, you see how most of my school years without any encouraging words or recognition of my efforts were fraught with this constant drawing blood by teachers and administrators, TRYING TO PROVE THAT I WAS INFERIOR, and , my trying to **survive** in the midst of it. None show you love, or belief in your abilities. It's a big cat and little mouse game. I have never earned a label from them that I was a noninterested or boisterous student. No, I never gave them reason to hate me or treat me as they did. I am very quiet; I do my work, but when they give me F for it, I come home crying and feeling very down in the world. My father builds up my spirit, always. He showed me a lady on television: Marian Wright Edelman who runs the Children's Defense Fund in Washington, D.C. And he's made me remember her words: "Education is our survival".

From my early years I got the idea America has a protective system and laws to watch those who get out of hand, so, why not watch the teachers more? All students who attend school regularly, who do their homework _should be passed in school._ There should be no giving Fs to those students. My father says the failure is the teacher's failure, not the child's. I believe: all students who are serious about their schooling should be allowed to stay in school, even college, and go as far as their minds tell them they want to go. Too many biased people are telling us: we can't do this; we can't do that! The old grading system has to be thrown out! as it allows all those too-impatient , too-judging teachers with bad feelings about categories of so-called underclass people to get even, in their sick way, with the society they identify as the child's. It gives them too much power TO KILL THAT CHILD BEFORE HIS LIFE BEGINS!

In a free country, all men who want to move ahead and improve themselves should have the opportunity (without harsh grading before they even get a good start). Such encouragement is particularly a must as a young person finishes high school and is at that crossroad where he needs support to have the best future possible. Too often superior-thinking teachers will not help an LD child anywhere upward! They discourage his going to college. He should be satisfied with something lowly. Now, once he gets into college, the snubbing and mistreatment is immediate and gross! While being admitted, you have to take placement tests, to be judged again, and usually they put you in basic skills classes which are nothing but a vague repeat of high school and pre-high school courses. And you can't get out of that until the new woman says you can. So, you do not really enter college on **equal terms** with the others. You are pushed back into some limbo-land which is not college, and they hold you there because they are getting college pay to keep you there! The normal kid gets admitted, and he can take any courses he wants to, and he moves ahead earning credits towards graduation. Not so the LD child. They want him there much longer! He is faced with:"You can't do this"; "You can't do that." He has no control over planning or progress.

Usually bad judgment, or, downward judgment of his past is very evident. The system does not make college teachers behave better toward the LD student. You may have to spend as much as twelve hours a week in these basic skills classes and get not one credit for them, yet, your parents have to pay fully for such courses as if they were credit-earning. Some colleges even charge extra for having the learning disabled child there in the first place. And in my case, the first person to snub me was the Learning Disabled woman who began immediately mouthing her You-Don't-Belong-Here syndrome. That syndrome , incidentally, is a part of the scam at college level: to take the money of LD kids then hold them in limbo-land just like the Haitians were held at Guantanamo. Too often in American institutions the superior thirst goes unchecked. In our prison system and in our education system as well, the greedy game of control flourishes with all its evils. Certainly hypocrisy and thievery in the teaching game needs cleaning up in this category where we LD students (and minorities) are abused.

In the stone above certain libraries it says that books are the wealth open to everybody. If this is true, then the system should allow us to educate ourselves where schools are so biased they exclude us! In other words, diplomas and degrees for homestudy. Even men in prison know that it is rather fruitless to try to strangle the cellmate. Teachers too should realize it's a tight little world, we LD people and dark-colored people are a part of it. We want our chance to move ahead. Why does the system allow those with the titles to malign us? I believe their untamed flaw is excessive pride in Self, and dearth of a desire to take in new knowledge from the underclass, to learn beyond the clichés, and to serve Americans broadly.

In America we have respected this royalty of station, this grouping off of those with the credentials, taking power over us. Look at the mess in the health-care system and all the terribly-padded bills in hospitals, charging people five dollars for an aspirin while every staff doctor thinks he deserves to own a Mercedes or Cadillac! We've allowed a first loyalty to be with this grouping off, and that's also a part of the deficit problem, I am told. Our future gobbled up by the greedy. Well, I've been very lucky in my young life. I was born of gentle parents. In foster care I learned religious life. And, with my new father who has taken me to some twenty countries, I have learned a first-hand view of the whole world's people. I have enjoyed being with people of different cultures, different backgrounds, and I think Americans have a lot to learn from those even in developing nations who are gentle souls. In places around the world where people have little in material wealth, they do show a respect for each other, and they seem to live happily not overpowering their fellowman. Many teachers in America have joined the class of <u>overbearing</u> people who try to overpower the little man, or, the child without a proper family. **You judge him, and you strike him down!** Around the world I saw happy people, each with his trade or his skill which he could proudly do, without interference. I'm merely trying to get that far, and in a country like America, it seems almost impossible for me.

In America, with our severe groupings , we have lost respect for the little man. We are ready to mistreat any who do not fit into our shell, or, over whom we have control. And we misjudge when we classify such people. Yes, I've seen humble people living with compassion, progressing without so much schooling. But as an American, I want that schooling, the same as the next American!

And I refuse to keep quiet when biased teachers mark me F for all of my good works!

Staying with my subject, I say: people with power have a tremendous thirst to gobble up little powerless people, and all the religions have not dissuaded them. We the common people have managed to stay alive by wiggling like worms in a basket, wiggling to get to the top, to breathe some fresh air. . . not to be crushed by others. Those who carry the basket would eat all the bread, all the fish. Now , how did I get to worms , bread and fish? It may have something to do with my love of reading the Bible (when I see no way out among men). Also, my mind is not perfect, but I'm convinced it is as good as the next man's, while in my schooling, white teachers and white administrators have marked my records and me so far downward, that it is clear they want me remembered as somebody inferior, inferior, inferior. Invariably and unfortunately teachers marking me hardest have been Jewish teachers. Dad cautioned me against saying this, but I think it is very important. I've thought many hours for an insight as to why this has happened, and I'll give you my views toward the end of my book.

I decided to do this book when several nasty teachers and administrators at my college (Westchester Community College) discounted all of my good work and decided to give it the lowest grade, mainly to teach my father and me our lowly place in the world. When we went to the dean we got no help from him. The die was cast and they would dishonestly discredit me this way, and there was no recourse, no redress. As the LD woman had said that very first day with her that I did not belong there, here's reason certainly to give me my money back! And give me back my reputation! Let me get away from you! No, they string you along, never admitting their cruel game. And, academic people love to say that everything is the student's fault. Here there was certainly negative collusion of the worst sort among teachers and administrators sticking together behind the predictions and edicts of an LD woman who **was never going to help me**. Her racism would be cloaked under the term 'professional judgment'. My file showed her I was a child of foster homes, somebody born with some brain damage, somebody Spanish, now with an adoptive father , a Black (to them), who poses to be highly-educated and wealthy! Excellent game for the evil - doers. The LD specialist's main thought was :_Hold Back This Inferior Student._ Me, so hopeful and alone on that beautiful campus. When

18

suddenly we were charged by this wild animal atmosphere, we found an academic bureaucracy ready to chew us up. We had no powers to stop such a negative dynamo from going into motion. That precisely was a climate in America where racism can and does blossom, grow and thrive. LD status coupled with race! All LDs and minorities can be equal captives, but I stress, the Black or Puerto Rican can tell this story better than a white LD kid. Nevertheless, we both need government help to stop and correct the wicked controlling of our lives, the **manufacturing** of bad records for us not to succeed.

My argument to you, why should any decent school allow these not-so-decent teachers to thrive in their midst? They've taken me, a young man with a very good mind, and made me mincemeat within four months! My earnestness to learn was thrashed! Did marking me down as a failure mean efficiency in their work? Absolutely not! They were delinquent to the nth degree. But nobody cares. *Education should not be a big, dishonest bureaucracy.* Somebody should care that we each are given the best chance at education. What I was given was worse than pig slop. I alerted my two college presidents; they did nothing. Next, the Federal Government should turn the screws and make college professors and administrators **more responsible.** When they treat people like they've treated me, make them squirm, each of them. Make them accountable whenever they fail a student! Thus, government could perhaps grasp control over some college wickedness, and be on the right track to improving America's higher education. Certainly it should stop this folly of failing grades for people you do not like. In the teaching game of prejudice the country pays the price. I was born to serve. **Let me serve.** Teachers, so far you've gotten away with your false judgments of me. Your cruel ploy is to consider some of us as not worthy of going forward. With such ideas, you're not ideally American. I saw you almost killing yourselves to make sure I didn't go anyplace upward! You'll even argue that your mischief is to **keep the standards high**, that you do everything right in failing "*one of them!*" Not an ounce of compassion, nor any weakening, where racism rules!

It mattered not that I was a very good student at high school, finishing with regular diploma, several awards of honor, and 85%-90% average. The racist game (for LDs) discounts all of that. At WCC they had me starting anew as an Inferior, with nothing to do but follow their prison demands of me. Ugly urges played with finesse.

19

How do I know? The English was blatant; I'm no fool. Oh, for a tape recorder! When my new father saw their dishonest downgrading of me, then in the end those horrible failing grades, after my good performances in classwork (which he followed daily, and he is not a dumb man), he knew there was nothing left to do but fight them. But *you're weak alone!* To convince others of the needs, we'd keep alive the subject, as surely they'd do it again to a good, unsuspecting kid who came there to learn and to pass. Such dishonest offerings of only low grades tend to discredit the teaching oath. It's misuse of public funds, but try to prove it; the cards are all stacked against you. If we LD students and minorities are fair game for such wreckless killing, we still have a voice , and I say Government should (a) recognize that such wickedness is rampant, and (b) outlaw it by closing the doors that allow it to happen. Especially education at the college level needs cleaning up. Those schools which are not private should not be allowed to get away with such treatment and exclusion. Ladies and gentlemen, no LD student, no progressing student, **Nobody attending school every day deserves all Fs.** If such is put on a transcript, there should be an investigation, and by all means, a way to remove such Fs, to wipe the slate clean!

We, my father and I, only saw the Learning Disabled so-called professor , so-called mentor for me, for *one short hour* that semester. That was at mid-terms. In the first five minutes of our meeting she tersely said I didn't belong there, then delightedly said I was failing in everything (which wasn't true). But in her command she had been on the phone saying negative things about me FROM MY FILE, since she had never met me before the meeting. Likely, when her assistant told her the high level of the black man who was my father, she just couldn't resist the temptation to do evil, and began all her negative work against me.   Immediately in our meeting she declared I could not read or write, and I read and write very well! I read books, magazines, newspapers *daily,* and spend more than one thousand dollars a year in reading and listening materials. I won two writing awards in high school. *She discounted all this, insisting I didn't belong there.* Then, stupidly, she contradicted herself saying that since my father was 'able', I should plan to spend 'nine or ten years' there, that certainly I could never graduate in two or four years. Nine or ten years for a two-year degree? My father and I exchanged glances. There's no way in the world I could be that stupid. This woman , to me, acted like a   half-American ', i.e., with so much

20

venom against me, an **equal** American. I also felt she was like somebody only recently in middle-class. Her crude behavior before me suggested that, i.e., so much lack-of-knowledge racially or socially speaking. She could have been Polish, Jewish or Slavic; it didn't matter; she was clearly somebody ignorant of me and my world. Ignorant of how to behave! I saw in her racism of the worst kind. (A died-in-the-wool racist to me is someone who works diligently on the surface to make everything of her complaints look like real professional talk, an honest appraisal of me, my flaws, my faults.) What saddened Dad and me, the assistant LD woman, who up till now had been very nice to us, now froze and became unfriendly and took up the stance of her boss! Later Dad said the LD woman's disrespectful constant bottom-talk of me, her exaggerations, was the manner of a racist. But how could we rise above that? How could we fight it?

Leaving that office, I felt very faint, very low, very betrayed. Almost as if I'd been brutally attacked physically. And I was so disappointed in her assistant for not offering the meeting one good word about me. I remembered all her former smiles, now gone. She was like a new recruit to racism, and Dad said it could spread that way. People fearful of their jobs. Mainly I felt the bigoted LD woman, the teachers who had failed me, all of them, should not be allowed to practice such abuse, especially over students they're charged to help. And America must learn to fight their misuse of power, if our institutions of learning are to remain whole. Fight them like roaches, Dad did say in a light moment when he was not completely down in his suffering for me.

The woman knew nothing about my physical weaknesses, and she really didn't care. Her aim was to pull me down in a general fashion, to crucify me! She spoke a steady shocking diatribe against me (which she'd never likely do before a white child or a white parent). She wouldn't listen to any details my father had to offer. She was the queen! She knew everything. And she likely had in preparation for this meeting urged my teachers to consider that I was inferior and unworthy. Her evil messing around was to damage me in such a way that I could not continue college there. All this wronging, yet in the calm American system, it could happen and I'd merely become a wash-out, another low statistics of an inept Black or Spic who didn't belong in "our college" in the first place.

21

As I left there I knew that my chances at this school, or any other, had been ruined. Just by the evil behavior of one or a few. In deciding to fight it, we dropped our vacation and began counting our finances we'd need for a lawyer. And her behavior would tie me up completely as to getting a college education anywhere else soon! It was a grave moment in my life. And it came so suddenly, so unannounced. And just as I was worrying most, the idea came to me to write this book. It was about all I could do of a positive fashion. It would prove I could write, I could read, that I did have academic promise, that I did have my wits about me. Most of all, it would prove my interest in college, and when a person pays his fees and has my interest, he should not be turned away.

Dad told me a book would be a tremendous undertaking in time and effort. He did notice how sad I was, like someone who had had a dozen eggs smashed in his lap. I confessed I was confused now, as I knew precisely it hadn't been my fault. Dad too knew because he is always with me and always watching me studying. This misguided woman probably thought I'd quit school, go out somewhere in the Ghetto, drinking beer, gambling, drugs, wasting my life. (" _They all do it," I can hear her say._) And her role in my future would be something like a doctor giving arsenic as a prescription. All their attitudes seemed to say: God has appointed me to kill this kid and his father. It was that simple what we saw at WCC. Yes, they openly wanted to keep me from my schooling.

"Dad," I kind of whined. "I _can_ write the book if you help me. I want to! The truth must be told."

He looked at me a long time, then he reached out and hugged me. "Go for it!" he exclaimed. Then he warned me that it would be very hard work, more than I had ever done before. And he'd be a slavemaster over me! I said Okay; I'm ready to work! I'd spend more than seven months writing notes and getting my thoughts on this horrible experience down on paper. I didn't think I could ever finish. My hands ached. I got headaches. I took aspirins, vitamin C. It was not easy reliving these ideas of evil which happened to me just in four short months, or eight, and in one horrible one-hour racist meeting of lies and insinuations. But I am happy now. I have tried my best, and I have something to show for my efforts. Perhaps the book won't clear my educational slate, but it has given me confidence in my ability, my purpose in life. But we should not in the American

22

system let an evil bunch in the teaching game ruin our transcript records, our future. All that dishonesty. Maybe it was joy for them!

But now I'm learning the spiritual world, and I know somehow things will even up for me. And I believe all the evil ones trying to hold back those of us who are minority and learning disabled, holding us back because they can get away with it. . . some day they will pay. Yes, I believe that. People really dedicated to teaching would **never** scar a person this way. The good ones don't even see color, they don't even see:Learning Disabled. We're all equal Americans.

Many charged with helping LD students think that we are of lesser families who will accept anything, never seeing the evil intent. They want to create for us an iron collar of detention, and a permanent record of lowliness, of failure. Why? To soothe one's power , not especially to punish, but power to be somebody big and important. That thirst for superiority (while treating others as morons) is especially evident. While in high school and middle school I was annoyed by arrogance among special ed people. Perhaps this is mainly a big city problem, but I still don't understand how people who chose teaching can behave that way.

In my case, Dad and I knew that the real issue was him. Many whites are not comfortable meeting a rich Negro, one of high culture, of mixed blood, whose family had been high up in American politics for more than 150 years. It confused them. And you would think it would have nothing to do with me, my education. But it does have.   Since education is: CONTROL TO THE FUTURE. They thought I should have all my lowliness brought out, to stop my progress, or, just to make it difficult for me to advance. I can hear them saying about Dad:" This nigger thinks he's so important. I'll fix it so his son can never finish college, so there!"

If you can make yourself take a look at the structure of education, you'll understand how racism can creep in. Teachers are people working alone in stuffy rooms. They sit and ponder over student papers.   When grading time comes, they also think of whether or not they like that kid. Then the grade goes down. Is it honest? Sometimes not. Now take the office of the LD woman. She sits there being boss over us. She wants to see us or control us, and since she never got her hands on me, this was an outrage. But her assistant had done very well with me. . . we worked together nicely, day after day. But the reports going over from the assistant to the main lady included somebody else. My father. And he was the

23

poison they had to deal with. A quiet unassuming man, but one all serious in seeing I get the education the government says I am entitled to. To her, HE was the obstructionist! She'd first brand me as *No Good*, then oppose anything he'd offer for me. No, what she really did was concentrate on *My File* . Take it under a microscope. . . *look for anything and everything she could criticize of me.* Is this the proper atmosphere for education? Absolutely not. Striking back with venom makes some people feel good. But the godly know that ignorance, resentment and fear are also a part of racism. Americans tend to concretely think: all blacks are poverty and ex-slavery. And many think they should exist *under* white Americans.

In the first place, my new father's family were none of that background. They've been wealthy university people for more than a hundred years. And successful business people longer than that. Their culture outshines the culture of many upper-middle-class pure whites, and this generation is about the seventh or eighth generation of that family's good fortune. History books don't teach you that such people of color had a place in old America. Now I'm in that family and I have a mission too. Dad tells me that it would be a rare thing for an upper-class white boy to be treated as I was by my teachers. No, they think more of the white boy's background. And they will give him more in the bargain. The big issue, whites coming up tend to fight the Black who has too much in their estimation. The way the LD woman snapped at Dad, it was unnatural, showing so much abhorrence. And he had done nothing to make her behave that way. Yes, it was a mystery, a mystery involving me and my future. For me, Dad says, it will always be a harder road. . . more proof before getting the pudding! As a man of letters Dad knows that racism is growing in America. When one's chances get marred by it, as it's happened to me, I guess I have to live through it as a soldier lives through a battle. And, it's meant that I have been put in a position forcing me (the quiet one) to fight.

Shortly after adoption I learned that Dad's family is as white as any Puerto Rican family. His people's roots are mainly in Europe, not Africa. His maternal grandmother was part-Cherokee and part-German. His father's family are Scotch-Irish with a touch of Negro blood. I have met his European kin from Sweden and Denmark. White people don't know that there are such connections in black families. He is brown while most of his relatives are fair. He claims he learned a lot about racism right in his own family. His four

24

university degrees didn't come easy. But he got an early start, in the University of Michigan at age 16. When he was my age, just reaching twenty, he was in the U.S. Army. It was segregated then. His white colonel in the Air Corps had his records stamped 'white' because Dad had made 165 IQ on Army tests and the colonel said that was too high for a colored guy, "stamp his records 'white'!".

With so many white-faced relatives Dad doesn't cringe at so-called white people, he either takes them or leaves them for their friendliness, or stupidity. He's never had to think race because of the great mixture of his family. Yet, when he meets some as rude as the WCC woman, it throws him completely out of his secure position. She treated him as a farmhand. He worried in this case because her attacking certainly meant something harmful to me. Her exaggerating to make me a failure was bad, but worse was all the negative talk right in front of me! He felt it would hurt my self esteem.

So Dad's Army service was partly in the white army and partly in the segregated regiments for Negroes. He was very flexible. His thoughts were individualistic rather than racial. In New York during World War II he gained further training in intelligence, and was recognized for his fluency in Italian and German, as a brown-faced man who could be very useful to the U.S. Army. And he did serve them well. When time for him came to leave the specialized training group in New York , he was to go to the 34th Infantry (white) in Mississippi, but he then asked his white colonel to stamp his records 'colored' so that he could stay out of Mississippi. This was done and he then joined the 92nd Infantry Division (black) in Arizona. Overseas he served as a linguist on the Italian front, and interrogated German and Italian prisoners on the Front and in prison camps. As a teenager at Michigan some professors gave him a rough time there, but he returned to his beloved Ann Arbor after the war (after music and business law studies in Florence, Italy), and earned a liberal arts bachelor's degree . He had already earned a pre-war Michigan diploma in mechanical engineering under government auspices, in which he served as a war materiels specialist. After the war and his Michigan bachelor of arts degree, he started a business, wrote a book, then went on to Columbia University, completing a master's degree in public law and government , seconding in languages. As soon as he completed his course requirements for the Ph.D. in international relations, he took himself into United Nations work where he remained for over thirty years.

Dad had explained to me that his future was never certain. In college over ten years, he prepared himself in several fields (including education, languages, literature, music, engineering, and as a political scientist). He had had setbacks for being a `first' at many things, arriving in the executive world some two decades before others of his race were accepted there. It meant learning methods of fighting racism. Yet, in his career at UN he had been a Far East and a technical assistance specialist. Nothing to do with American racism. Gentile and erudite, he would baffle my college teachers. Now he feels largely what I have suffered has been because of him, and how those tricky teachers interpret our lives. On stage: their negative appraisals of _Me,_ (a puzzle-toy), with . . everybody ready (with green envy bag) to dramatize my (our) unworthiness.

The LD supervisor at WCC was probably used to calling the shots when she met with a minority family, parents of a slow learner. At the outset of the meeting she snapped at Dad, telling him he had to listen to "two professionals". When he told her quietly that he too was a 'professional', she turned purple. Then she proceeded to make my name mud. He objected quietly, by interjecting with good things about me. She pretended not to hear them; then she'd squirm, then bite out more disgusting words, trying to make him a nothing and me a nothing.

Well Dad felt he certainly should report the incident to higher officials, but when he did, they stuck together like worms. In his quiet manner, he fought back for me; he knew their wicked thirst. They were trying to waste my life, unjustifiably. I was scared, I was fearful, but I knew **I had done nothing wrong**, and I was proud of him for fighting to save my life. The alternative. . . I could go home, quit college (as she suggested), get a lowly job, and go on with life. _BUT THAT WASN'T ME!_ **I had looked forward to college, and, I had deserved to be there.** Why should I let any of them run me away? Dad pondered: if he didn't come on campus, would I have a better chance? He didn't come often, maybe once a month. No, in our case, everything was _a game of exaggerations,_ The various complaints, it was truly a way of getting rid of me. Maybe I didn't have to go to college, but the decision should be ours, and not forced on us by racist dishonest people. Furthermore, he was the only one who knew how hard I studied, and how much progress I had made, enough to merit 'passing' in any honest school.

As that meeting ended Dad was sad for me; he knew this woman charging like a hound had set the race against me; the traps had been baited to ruin my life. He offered his hand at the close of the meeting but she wouldn't accept it. Truly , we had never seen in education a person with so much venom, and, we believed, she'd go to no ends to stop me in my educational aims.

I could now see her as a young student, and I guess she, on her graduation day, felt she was going out into the world and really be a help to LD students. But in her attitude you had a feeling she was thinking black and white , superior and inferior. . .help some but not help all. So why pick me as a one you would not help? the one you would malign? I am still trying to figure that out completely, but I would need a course or two of psychology and sociology. With the setup for LD students you first must take remedial work (basic skills) before they'd let you into anything as interesting as sociology or history. This too is a flaw of judgment and prejudice. All of us LD students who have graduated from high school, need a fair chance to start college without all these conditions. But the _tag of inferiority_ is something they like to work with. Something they want you to feel and never forget.

So you see, my story is mainly a story of misuse of power. _TO KILL!_ As I am writing my notes I am listening to a TV program on abortion and the lady is saying"why would you kill a child you can save?". . . "unborn children who are helpless". . ."children only have value after birth". . . "that 's a religious, a moral issue". . ."we've got to hear what the other people say". . "give us a chance to try it" . The last statement stuck in my mind. At WCC I was never given a fair chance; evil forces were at work. And, when I finally left there, my life wasn't really over. I had swallowed disappointment before. Now with my new dad I was learning how to fight those evil forces who have all the power. You walk very quietly, and speak with diplomacy. And you look around for cohorts. (This is another new word.) This search has brought me knowledge for which I will not get credit in my transcript. Perhaps it will help me one day to finish up my education and get a job. That's what we all want, but when they stop you cold with "you must repeat this; you must repeat that", it seems we are in an unending muddy marsh. I want to get out. I want to free myself.

Quietly in a diplomatic way my father tried to search out some favorable persons on the WCC campus, but everybody he met was afraid to stand against the evil ones, and mostly they were unduly proud of their station; the student was a tool in their hands. The system had taught them to be confident of their position, of their power. And the team spirit among that campus' teachers was to make it almost impossible for a plagued student to get any redress. Their control was completely golden, for them.Yet, one would hear a lot of complaining from black students (who were mostly under Financial Aid). They said many teachers treated them as inferiors. And in grading. Favorite status was given to the whites and to Asians. In the cafeteria I'd listen to the grumbling blacks, wanting to tell them my story. Maybe together we could start a revolution there. Well, most of them were not LD students. Maybe they had a better chance than I did, nobody pointing out an indelible record of their inferiority, or any need for them to be given an F grade unjustly. Whites on that campus were more relaxed; they had time for socializing, and clubs, but to me they did not seem very studious. Perhaps they didn't have to be; I knew they were getting the good grades, and eventually the degrees. Racially I didn't belong in either group, and I had thought I had an umbrella of support in the campus' nicely-equipped LD office, but I was completely wrong. That office was my undoing.

WCC is a state-supported school and any such school supported by public funds should not have a teaching staff so proud of itself, and so prejudiced against minority and LD students. Individual students need protection from biased teachers, but if you were the right color, the right class, maybe you could go through that school with no trouble, until graduation. But for the iron collars they'd stick on some of us, there'd be no escape. Yes, I felt some there could have a matter of luck, and they could graduate with their color and think no racism existed. But it is the _Some of Us_ who don't get by the rigorous screening, the some whom they feel need taming, it is us America needs to worry about. We are not free people in such schools. We are not getting our share. Please make the system foolproof, so they can't play around with the some of us.

That school with its mossy grass lawns, its Hartford mansion, its yellow-stone buildings, its fine library and many offices with modern equipment, doesn't particularly need a Learning Disabled specialist who is not there to help each and every one of the LD

28

students. Not on her terrible terms and tactics, but treating us first as human beings, with rights and certainly with good behavior and progress on our side. Her terrible biased judgment of me meant, to me, that the system needed more rigid controls on people's fantasies of superiority.

On the day after our short meeting she banished my father from campus. This was a shock. Now how could I do well with such behavior to him? All parents want to be regarded as honorable people. But you can't be with a racist! And for me it would mean no one on campus speaking well of me. We soon told the Dean but he was no help. He never scheduled a meeting to see us, never knew me other than what the biased whites on his staff had told him. What was trumped up by that scheming LD woman, who hated my father more than she hated me, never got a hearing. We were left with nothing for our money but a horrible negative transcript for me to try to carry forward . I knew in my mind I was a good and viable student. I learned a great deal while at WCC; learned much of it from my books (by myself), from my private tutors, and from my father. Practically nothing from the WCC teachers. They gave me the Fs, never showing me or my father any papers of failure, and I knew I had some As there on my class papers, all forgotten once the evil woman took over. And this would be my record long after all of them were dead!

Our beautiful country home on the Hudson is chocked full of reading materials which both my father and I enjoy. I enjoy being a well-traveled person of culture. But as yet I am prepared for no job, and I want to be. I think often of that American white woman , controlling me in the teaching game, who declared dishonestly: HE CANNOT READ OR WRITE. I think about those others in the teaching game who accepted what she manufactured as the gospel truth. This clear racism if ever put to a test involves an atmosphere and a situation of judgment. Any retesting for me could be set up in a flaky or dishonest manner. Americans should realize that many matters of judging achievement of minority students are flanked with outright bigotry. My reading is clear and steady; sometimes I may hesitate around certain words, yet, teachers exaggerate my reading disability (often stopping me while I am reading aloud and well, and confident of myself). Of course, I'm not Richard Burton, and neither are they! In writing I am a bit slow (owing to my muscle coordination problems) but I have made steady improvement and am certainly not a failure at it. My spelling and lettering are very good. What I am telling you here, when they judge you, they judge you against _the Best._ My reading vocabulary has improved tremendously, enough for me to have a passing grade. How can I say this? I work at my weaknesses all the time, and God knows the time I spend and the improvements I've made merit recognition. White teachers do not give you proper merit for your achievements. The system needs fair judges! And I don't need a biased woman saying I can't read or write who has NEVER TESTED ME.

Mainly, they should have considered that I am blind in one eye, and no blind or half-blind person is ready on the pick-up exactly like sighted persons. Also, I had no mother tongue in infancy (being moved constantly between English-speaking and Spanish-speaking houses). Now I don't want you feeling sorry for me, but how can teaching people (with microscopes) judge part of your life, never looking at your achievements and circumstances, and with no grasp or concern of your total life? And it would perhaps be nice if they really cared. But they don't, yet they can x my future all they please!! I ask you, how many other students fit my situation? Can't I be praised a little for what I have accomplished? I knew, in college, I had to remain respectful to imbecilic people who deep down inside thought of me as a moron whom they could play with, viz., pick fault and limit me. Injure me, and throw me on a garbage heap! And that would be America's loss. I am a good person, as good as they are! If you talk to God, He will tell you that.

Not to have a completely negative transcript, we wrote to the New York State Dept. of Education asking if there were a review panel. Dad was confident I could show my comprehension skill and mastery of words, spelling and writing if before an impartial body or a Court. Unfortunately, no such redress exists. The schools are allowed to be completely omnipotent, and their teachers can get away with such outlandish prejudice and bigotry, stealing my time and good name. Now we are working with civil rights people and the U.S.Dept. of Justice, and maybe soon I shall have the chance to prove I can read and write satisfactorily. With proper safeguards in the national education system, this time-consuming injustice would have no more space to exist. Government may consider that one poor student's life isn't worth much, but I think quite a few good people are killed off as I have been. Mainly, not even one innocent man should go to prison! And a prison is what they've put me in.

My high school had said I was pretty good at computers, or, that I had an aptitude for computers, so I was very glad when Dad agreed I could try out his new Zenith computer with my ideas for this book. First we sat together in our beautiful computer room lined with colorful Haitian paintings (it had been our dining room). First Dad helpfully would talk and draw out of me ideas about my youth, my school experiences. And I'd take a few notes. And I'd also look into one of my dictionaries to check on words he spoke that I did not know. (I own five dictionaries, including my Webster's and my Oxford.) Dad told me just to put down ideas as they came to me, and to stay organized, and thinking about my goal. (He loves that word: 'organized'!) Teachers too would harp on me for not being 'organized'. I guess that's what I missed in my early years without parents to guide me. Dad (who adopted me seven years ago) told me further to express myself and try to keep people interested. Well, last night I watched a television show on *Nature*. It was about Russia, about how animals survive in the cold of Siberia. Beautiful Russian eagles build their nests high up; and two fuzzy-white chicks have to share that nest. As it so happens, the bigger of the two constantly pecks at the baby chick. The little one, peeping loudly, scurrying frantically, trying to scamper away. TO SAVE HIS LIFE. And the parents don't try to help him. Soon he is killed by the bigger chick. This happens, they say, in 75% of the nests. I think about those lucky little fellows in 25% of the nests, who survive. Now, we humans behave just as badly, not letting downtrodden people survive. I want to be among the 25%. Yes, we hear a lot about Human Rights, but usually we are thinking about some faraway places, not home. Yes, we do peck at people, killing them! I want you to know the treatment against the Learning Disabled is a killing game. If the government provides for us, it must realize we are not inferiors and it should not tolerate teachers who treat us this way. So many people with the jobs want to be like the blood-thirsty eagles, consuming the weak. Being so greedy, all their defensive words of protection are merely sham nothingness. They should be helping us to come up, but they give up on us, giving us nothing. . . and, very often , PUSHING US DOWN!

My life has been a scurrying not to be crushed by greedy people armed with their jobs and titles, ready to grade me, possess me, floor me. They eat all the bread. I've always loved school and learning , and in it, I've suffered so much misery and misjudgment. Why? Daily I've attended to my duties and tried to learn, and I do learn, but I get no credit for it. Why? Because I am slower than other students. The government has told them that I should be allowed to come along at my own speed, but no, they won't have that; they'll count me out, and I am not to peep in my defense.

In my search for identity , like many teenagers, I've taken to the Rock n' Roll culture for some identity. Dad makes me wear my hair neatly but I am allowed to wear black t-shirts and jewelry with crossbones and skeletons on them. Dad thinks this is why some teachers have graded me badly, but I must shout for my share of freedom. Now I'm reading a lot about the parapsychological world. As I'm now learning about other people's minds, I see more clearly this devilish urge to control and destroy, by a group who are not more normal than the rest of us. Teachers with ulterior motives! I've told my Jesus I'm not going to let them destroy me. I won't let it happen to me.

My freedom at the moment is to tell what teachers and administrators have done to me, and let you be the judge (so that it does not happen to your loved-ones). I should let you in on a secret: most of us who have been in special classes for slow children mainly want to be with the rest, and treated like the rest.   This seldom happens.   Teachers and administrators are not that concerned or humanitarian.   They like having us in a straitjacket. We want to achieve and measure up, and society should help us measure up. Your society allows the teachers and the administrators with their titles to have too much sway over our lives. You must check them as government supervisors are supposed to check how wardens take care of prisoners. Or, better still, how Army officers check their troops. My father's told me he learned a lot about orderliness and fairness while serving four years in the Army during World War II. I got my exposure to military regimentation by being three years in the Boy Scouts. I liked it. It was good for my mind, but I don't think they'd ever take me in the U.S. Army with my one blind eye, and with my muscle coordination problem, my little speech defect, and my huge nevi scar (five feet long), my birth scar. Well, Dad always says none of us is perfect. But he shares my great desire to have an education, and he says he, while a colored man, was never deterred as I have been deterred by teachers, i.e. because of my various disabilities.

Dad's taught me to be a fighter. I am still shy in setting out to do things (after so many years of being told I am inferior), but I am no longer shy in my efforts, or in spotting a treacherous so-called teacher-hypocrite. Some teachers are good, of course, but it is difficult to sway them from their opinions of who you are! Soon after adoption I had a newly-found self esteem . The teachers regarded this as a kind of impertinence , and only few encouraged me in my new enthusiasm for life. They would not let me get away with my budding spirit, my newly-found freedom to be an individual. I had to find courage to withstand **them**!

The big lesson most learning disabled children learn at school is that they must defend themselves against all the negative talk from the teachers and staff. They must keep their parents involved. And the family should have an equal voice with the teachers. In talking to each other, we kids agreed that teachers are not perfect, and that their judgment of us makes a permanent record, but it should not **rule** us. These records often are spotted with prejudice and misjudgments. When the LD woman at WCC nastily began to try to kill me, all she knew about me was my records. We had spent no time together, but she was very ready to crucify me, to tell me I did not belong without speaking *ten minutes* to me as a person!

All of us LD kids, whether in grade school, high school or college, who regularly attend our classes and do our school work with enthusiasm, we can measure up if given the chance. (In fact, I think we could do so in regular classes not separated from the other students of our grade. But it would take a patient, understanding teacher. Most of them are very impatient and not understanding!) Those society appoints as our mentors are often bad eagles needing control. Society needs to watch how they use us to put more gold on their caps, leaving not a speck of gold for us.

***** ***** *****

33

CHAPTER THREE

Of my early years, the beginning, I remember feeling a pleasant warm tingle, sitting or lying awake in bright sunlight. I don't remember specifics of the people in my life. I do remember kitchen tables with food; people talking and walking around, the smell of candles or roach spray. A man or woman, bouncing me on their knee. My parents, I suppose. We were in different houses, different rooms. My memory began working quite nicely in my first days at kindergarden. I was so excited about the very idea of going to school, of learning things. And I was happy to be out in the world with other children. At school, in those big rooms, they would teach us beautiful things about flowers, trees, and animals. All the world seemed in harmony there. Never once did it come into my mind that there would be negative teachers one day, ready to think only bad things of me, trying to find a reason not to educate me.

My kindergarden teacher at P.S.77, Miss Cunningham, was very nice. She loved the kids and treated us all the same. She was white and we were largely mixed. This was in the Bronx, New York City, in the late 1970s. When I got to first grade it was a different story. The teacher, Mrs. Goldstein, was always frowning at me, pulling at my clothes, and she gave me Es. I cried because I knew this wasn't a good grade and I wanted to have good grades like the other children. My parents didn't keep much in contact with the school. They were too busy keeping food on the table. It seemed there was nobody to go to to make Mrs. Goldstein behave. The trouble wasn't me; I was polite and as nice as I could be. I did my lessons and tried to remain decent to her. Why, Lord, did she hate me? And, I was afraid to tell anybody how she behaved toward me!

Tears became a part of my school day. Then, maybe my prayers were answered, because, next, we had to move again. The reason was our rent was too high and we were on Welfare. I was happy about this move; a new school and a new teacher would give me a better chance to show what I could do. Now there were other problems in the family and soon I was taken away from home. I didn't know why and I didn't have a proper chance to say good-bye to my parents or to my older brother, Eric. I was in a seashell all alone! Maybe they, the social workers, had put me under foster care because of my disabilities. When Mom asked them for me, they said it would only be for 'an indefinite period.' The idea of being separated from my parents and brother made me very nervous. BUT IT HAPPENED. The government's way. All alone I was moved to Queens, and in this new house and new neighborhood they made me start school all over again. I still liked it, but without parents or friends, it was rather lonesome.

Richmond Hill was like being on the moon. So quiet at night! And I didn't know how far away I was from my loved ones. It felt like at least a thousand miles. I began saying hello to peanut butter, and sandwich bread. They were familiar in my life. It was a nice neighborhood, with houses, but the school P.S. 55 was something like a prison. Teachers were always yelling and kids would come running. The principal, Mr. Weissman, made us stand at attention like wooden soldiers. You could not bat an eye. It made me nervous because I thought I would wet my pants when all my muscles were so rigid. The foster care lady where I lived did not make us breakfast. I merely got two cups of hot coffee. But I was so eager for school, this eating business did not bother me. Yet, I knew like the other kids that the teachers would treat you badly the more they knew about your family life. And those of us who were not white, they doubly treated us badly.

Next, I had to move again. This time to South Jamaica. It seemed a poor untidy neighborhood, but I liked the school better because we had some colored teachers and they treated us fine. With some bad people in the neighborhood, I had to be careful about many things as I walked to school. But my mind was happy now. I was learning many new things.

I did not see my parents but there still was school, and I liked it. As most of my new teachers were good to me, I went on without difficulties, and soon I was in the fourth grade! In that time my parents were divorced and my father remarried. My brother now was also put in foster care. He hated it. My poor mother suffered the worse because she did not have a big supporting family like my father had. She was alone and not in good health. Like me. Mrs. Maraposa, with whom I lived, was a little like my mother, but she never smiled and never kissed me. There was another boy in the house. Nicky. He was a bit tough but I grew to like him. On

Sundays Mrs. Maraposa always took us to church. Her religion was Pentacostal. After a year or so, Mrs. Maraposa had been thinking of adopting me, but suddenly she changed her mind. The story the social worker told seemed to say I did wrong by playing with toys. I was approaching teen years and they wanted me doing other things. By that time I knew I was a bit slower than other children; the social worker often discussed me while I was in the next room, listening. I didn't want to move again! That was my great fear. I could give up playing with little toys, but I really had nothing else that was truly my own. Since my parents had been alcoholics it was feared that my brain may have been damaged at birth. Twice they put me in the hospital for tests, but both times the tests were negative. And I was allowed to come back home. I did know that I had one bad eye from birth, and the good eye was also weak and roving. I had a nice copper color like a Mexican, and some people said I was good-looking. But I really felt like the Elephant Man, because, I had, mostly hidden, a huge nasty birth scar called 'nevi', which ran the four-foot length of my body. Very brown and looking like burnt pizza. I was very embarrassed about this scar because it ran right up to my face (little bits of it). Doctors shook their heads when they examined me. One said it might turn into cancer. Another doctor made me smile. I liked him.

People looking me in the face often asked:"What happened to you?" They thought I had been burned. I just smiled and told them weakly that it was my birth scar. I also had muscle problems in my hands. Some teachers screamed at me, expecting me to write like other children. I tried. My writing improved but I could not ever write as fast as other children. This hurt in tests, and, in being judged!
And, for my little speech problem, they had me in extra sessions. Again I was being judged against children who did not have the same problems. One teacher, Mrs. Novak, made a game out of my pronouncing words. I liked her. (My habit was to say 'like-ted', and I still do it some ten years later!) The real problem, I had never learned grammar; never long enough with a teacher teaching grammar. Also the System which identified me as 'Spanish' always put me in foster care homes where no English was spoken, yet, my social worker had told them downtown that my particular parents were English-speaking, in spite of their roots and surname. So needing to know English at school and Spanish at home, I knew nothing correctly. I was embarrassed about this, but nobody put me

36

in a situation to correct it. It was merely assumed that I was 'Very Dumb'.

So I went along smiling, trying to communicate in both languages, and I felt I did pretty well at this. I was a happy child, within myself. I liked strolling around outdoors. I liked kids but I kept a bit distant from them, thinking they would laugh at my bad eyes , my speech, and my brown protruding birth scar. When I took my bath I'd study my body. (I had been hospitalized for a hicky once.) At the middle of my abdomen where the brownish birth scar was as thick as burnt pie crust, there had been some oozing, but I'd tell nobody, because maybe they'd start cutting on me. I just learned to keep very clean and use talcum powder on my body. Mrs. Maraposa told me not to worry about cancer, that cancer only came to old people. Also she said that whenever people questioned me about my birth scar, I could say I was burned, but it was better to be truthful: merely say it was from birth. In summers, I loved to go swimming but I didn't go swimming often because of my scar and the fact that they would not let boys wear a top shirt. In winters , when we had to wear sweaters, a teacher kept staring at me when I took my sweater off, because of the gingerbread-like scar rising out of my shirt and shoulders, up my neck. She treated me as if I had a disease. This hurt more than the taunting from kids because teachers are supposed to know things. Nevi is only a birthmark, nothing more.

I think those teachers judging me and giving me bad grades did so for a number of reasons including my scars. Black teachers were not apt to do this. Nor Spanish teachers (but we had so few of them!). In my own mind these racist teachers could take it or leave it, but I did not like this whole business of 'judging me'. Is that what schools are for? American schools? I am sure their low-grading of me was flavored with the matter of their not liking my Spanish heritage or the way I looked (just as it was flavored with low-judging of my home life). As you can see from what I am saying, I was growing less and less favorable about our New York schools and the role of the teacher; and this was a pity since school was *the best thing* in my life. White teachers are quick to say:"You need psychological help." No! THEY need psychological help. Get off my back, you New York bunch of phonies!! Go back to school, get more education,or, give up the job, the good money; go back to the suburbs where you live!

37

Now that I've got that off my chest, let me get back to my story. The good thing about my Jamaica years , in that dark, dirty slumlike area, I had a wonderful time at school. And I was smart enough to make it without psychological help, without special education and without my parents having to come to school for useless meetings. I and my colored teachers got along very well, and, I got along very well with most white teachers who were in that setup. It was only later when I was shifted to white suburbs that I began to have real trouble in school. I didn't change but the system judged me as being less prepared than the white ones. Some of this may be true but, ladies and gentlemen, I feel most of it was the OPPORTUNITY TO DO EVIL, to take potshots at me, A disadvantaged slow learner, a minority name to whom they've attached an exaggerated written profile of who I am and where I can go. I once felt it was all racism, but if you will recognize that this can and does happen to many Learning Disabled students , even those who are white, then you know that it is more than racism. It is improper treatment in a bad institutional system. I believe in big city education, bad teachers and administrators in the system (including LD teachers), will continue to abuse many deserving children whom they consider NOT PERFECT ENOUGH. They want to put us on a garbage heap.

I'd go to school in the mornings happy as a lark, then come home often in tears, either because some teacher had been unduly hard on me, or some kids had laughed at me. Usually it was the former. Remember, I was always interested in learning, and I always tried to do my best. In spite of all my problems, I felt normal, as normal as the rest of the kids. But as time passed, the bad reports on me were getting looked at, and they were growing. What hurt most was that teacher here and there who would pick at my file and then viciously add her twobits of bad medicine, saying I was not normal, and treating me as if I was not normal, *when I had done good in her class!* They were not doctors to say that, and how could they wipe out my progress? How could I escape such reports following me from school to school? And a few would pinch me or push me in the classroom, always with frowns, treating me as if I were nothing but dirt. One of them wrote in my file that I was "super sensitive". Whenever I came to talk to her, she never had time. I merely wanted to tell her a joke, to see if she would smile. As I had no family to listen to my troubles, often I felt very bad about myself, wishing at

38

times that I had not been born. But this was my secret. I'd tell nobody my feelings, for, if I did, they'd certainly have me under psychological help!

In July 1986, at birthday time, all of a sudden my father died. I learned that he was hit by a car while crossing the street. The very racist Bronx police got into the picture, and he was not treated properly at the hospital. Barely forty, and now he was dead. Some said he was under the influence of controlled substances, but I never believed that. He died of mistreatment. Yes. I was allowed to go to his funeral, and I saw once again my brother and my stepmother. My real mother had been hospitalized with a liver ailment and we did not see her at the funeral. This was very sad for me because I loved my family; they had been happy together, and I had known them to be good people. My father had had trouble getting jobs. I often went with him in his old car when he was jovially collecting old mattresses, to resell. And I was joyous whenever he played his trumpet, and he was good enough at it to make some money in bands. Maybe the drinking was their only problem, and nobody could help them with that. I felt that social workers had unjustly broken up our family , when all they needed to do was help him find a job. Yes, we could have survived if someone had thought nicely of us that way. Even when out of work Dad was jolly and cheerful, never complaining, always hopeful. He loved to work, and to collect things. He gave me a flute, and I treasure it even today. He always had wanted me to go up in the world. He never saw my little injuries. He wanted me to think positive. When I was only five, he'd sit me on his lap in the car and make me handle the steering wheel. "See, you're driving," he'd shout with a smile. Yes, he encouraged me and I felt so proud of being able to 'drive'. I was sorry that he and Mom had broken up. I was sorry that he was taken to Heaven so young. Only 45, but in many ways he was ancient and his life was fully over before his death. He was constantly trying to rebuild, for me to have it better. I knew those were his thoughts.

Soon after this, I was transferred to another lady way out on Long Island: Mrs. Bivona of Central Islip. She was a strict Peruvian who had four other kids under foster care. She'd haul us around in her station wagon while she bought many things. But not for us. They were things for her house: stereos, VCRs, washing machines. She'd take most of our money, even the pennies from our pockets. We kids felt she was only into foster care for the money she could make from it; this government thing was paying her better than any job. Her husband was merely a janitor, yet, she'd talk proudly as if she were a princess living a princess' life. School for me in Central Islip was not as good as it had been in Jamaica. Now I was mostly among white people and the white teachers were particularly nasty to me. They openly began to criticize my slowness (some saying so in class, in a way as to make the other kids laugh at me). Now I was beginning to have my own strength; I could hold my head up high. I had more brains than they ever imagined!

But now, my mind did begin to wander in school. When I was friendly with classmates, they said I was pestering them. Well, I didn't want to be depressed, and thinking about my family, I could be depressed. So many bad things had happened to us and I had nobody to talk to who really cared. I learned that my real mother had signed some papers which the social workers brought her. This meant that they could now put me up for adoption. My brother now was also in a foster care situation out on Long Island, but he did not want to be adopted. Eric was nineteen and I was thirteen. He felt in a couple of years he would be old enough to be out on his own; he didn't want any more non-family people in his life. No foster care. No social workers. I, on the other hand, felt that perhaps I could find new life among caring people who would take me in as part of their family. At least, that was what I was hoping for, and poor Dad always wanted me to live with hope.

During the autumn of 1986 they made me have my picture taken for the Blue Book the state puts out on children wanting to be adopted. They made up a flyer with a little story about me. Nothing bad, this time. People would see our pictures in these books, and ask for us. In the photo my facial scar did not show up. I looked pretty good. And what they said about me was kind of favorable. Well, I'd wait it out and see. My brother said I could always say `no'. Just about this time things really began to get bad at school. One teacher really didn't like me. She knew my home situation and she began manufacturing complaints about my work and my behavior at school. She said I was annoying a white girl. To punish me, it was recommended that I be taken out of regular school and be put into something called Special Education. In a way it was a punishment and in another way , they said, it was for my benefit. By my being slower than most of the class, they said they could no longer spend so much time on me. Well, other teachers went along, and even my

40

social worker! Really I couldn't say no; I had to start packing. Word spread among the other kids. They told me that special education was very bad: we'd be pulled aside and isolated with handicapped children, retarded ones, and no longer to be able to go to classes with our friends. And also, bad children were put in special education, and I had to be fearful of my well-being. Some sadness came over me; but what could I do? One nice teacher told me to think positive, that the special ed setup would make it possible for me to learn more, well, not really, but to ACHIEVE. That's a judgment word. I felt I was learning okay. As for the bad kids in special education, that one good teacher I talked to said I'd have to learn how to defend myself. Yeah, and in doing so, I might turn bad, as bad as I would have to be in a bad neighborhood in New York City. Lord, I was going backward! I knew it, all because **one** _racist teacher made herself controlling my life._ Now I wished that I was back with my nice colored teachers in Jamaica. They'd never do this to me.

During my few remaining weeks, I kept hearing stories about special education. Other than the bad kids there'd be those who were lazy and disruptive, and those who were visibly deformed and stupid-looking and stupid-acting. We'd be bunched together in a special room with no courses like gym, music or art. And all day long you'd be with one teacher. If she were bad, you'd suffer. Now I didn't want to go to special education, but I knew I had no voice. There was nobody who would talk for me, to get me out of it. No like-family teacher to explain it to me. I had to learn everything about it from the kids in my class. All the teachers had given up on me; none would help me; just one acquiesced (Dad gave me this word.); and the principal was only interested in getting back from the social worker all the necessary papers and forms, so that my record could go forward in a 'complete' state.

Just before that fateful day was to happen, God made it possible for me to also hear some good news. Several people had called Little Flower Children's Agency (who were responsible for me) making inquiries about adopting me. The way it's set up, I have a voice too. They had asked me my preferences. All kids ask for a two-parent family, and in my case it would also be somebody Catholic or Spanish. From what I had heard, the agencies all work in a rigid racial-religious frame; a few would weigh my feelings as well. I really had no rigid requirements. Like most kids, I wanted a family that was good people, with whom I could have a better life. Have some fun. As it developed, my social worker had a good idea of what kind of person I am and she worked carefully with other agencies to screen for the right people for me. I am grateful to Kathy for that. As it turned out , the one man put at the head of my list was alone in the world. He had a very warm personality, a sense of humor, athletic build, a very active person, a very academic person who was a musician and an artist as well as a political science scholar, a linguist, a churchman. He was born on July 8th, while I was born on July 7th. Also he was Anglican Catholic and not Roman Catholic. And again, he had Spanish people in his family, but he himself was not Spanish. He had just retired from a long career as a senior official at United Nations. He sounded very interesting, but now I wasn't even sure that I wanted to be adopted.

Depressed, mostly about the treatment I was getting in school, I began running away. I'd walk as far as I could, or, I'd take a bus and ride as far as I could. With my few pennies I'd get a coke or a hamburger, then as darkness came, I'd look for a hidden place to sleep, where there would be a bit of warmth. The nights were long and tearful. I asked Jesus why all this had to happen to me. I had tried to be a good boy. As I tried to get comfortable in sticks and grasses smelling of dog urine, I'd think of Mom and Dad, and of the bleek situation for me once I was taken away from them. America was not the land of the free as I thought it was. Right now, there was no warmth in my life. I didn't consider myself stupid, lazy or deformed. I didn't want to go into special education, but I had no voice. Teachers were horrible, and nobody seemed to care!

I ran away several times, mostly long before the idea of adoption came up. Usually I was getting away from bad circumstances at school or the foster homes where I had stayed. Now it was clearly the school matter. At first there was some adventure in it, then those long hopeless nights, with me lying on the ground all balled up like a squirrel, became miserable. I wanted something to happen, and usually the police would find me the very next morning. The Irish police on Long Island were not so bad. They'd bring me back to Mrs. Bivona. The social worker, Kathy Pearson, would come and she'd take me back to school, to that drab schoolroom where Miss Bacon didn't like me. I told Kathy teachers had too much power over us kids without families. I think Kathy understood, but she couldn't balk at the system. She too needed her job. Back in classes,

I began wondering about the one man who wanted to adopt me. Now that I was back, I'd be able to meet him because they had already scheduled a meeting for us to come together at the Brooklyn office of Little Flower Children's Services. They had told him I ran away, but he still wanted me. God, how little the Agency and the School knew about me! And they try to know every thing about everybody.

Christmas that year I was very sad. I got no presents; I had no one to talk to, yet, I was still expected to do good in school! All the rules! "You must do this; you must do that." And :"We'll judge you as harshly as we please." None of them would say 'Happy Christmas', and none of them would give me a dime. From what my social worker had told me about the man from the United Nations, I was eager now to meet him. He came from a mixed-blooded family, Scotch-Irish, German, Negro, Cherokee Indian. He considered himself 'multiracial' but I knew some in the society would call him `black' for that one bit of it in his background. But I knew he was a fighter for new ideas, and I liked that. They had quizzed me a lot on this racial business, but I really had no objection. They said he was once married but not now; he was also said to be rather rich. Mainly I wanted him to be a nice person interested in having me as a son. They quizzed me on his other drawback, the fact that he was very old. Sixty! I didn't mind that. I had been told that he was youthful-acting and supposedly in good health.

When I gave up on the idea of a two-parent family, it wasn't that I was desperate. I had learned something very valuable in all my school problems: it just takes **one person** to make your life bad or good, and I had a feeling this man would be a very good person for me. A good Christian human being wanting me as a son. Surely, Mrs. Bivona, the Central Islip foster care woman, didn't want me, like Mrs. Maraposa and the others before her. And I had to stop considering school my refuge as none of the teachers wanted me. And Kathy, my Little Flower social worker , she too didn't want me. All along I had been thinking of her as my best friend, but she didn't fight hard enough when that nasty teacher, Miss Bacon, decided to kill me by having me put in special education. No, Kathy should have kept me out of all this trouble, but she didn't really think of me as Her Charge (like God makes a family). She didn't do her full job. Well, maybe she did. She was more concerned about getting me out of Central Islip and into a permanent home and family. She had been a good person for me. I had to stop **feeling sorry for myself** and realize the good things, my potential, my ability to go upward in spite of them. Now I believe the real ugly thing, the troublemaker, was my FILE. I wish I could have taken it off that desk where I saw it, and burned it, completely! Yes, that I should have done! With the biased ones of white people acting fancy in their jobs, they had made that file the master element in my life. And with it they took pleasure in wasting my life. Like a criminal now, I felt I should make one last-ditch effort to get that file, and burn it, so that my life could have a new beginning.

At nights when I was sleeping, I was so fortunate to have Jesus at my side, and we'd talk. He told me I could have a good new beginning without that file. And Dad kept saying "Be Hopeful". Maybe now a new beginning was possible. I began rocking like a little baby as the tears burned my cheeks. Soon I was asleep, and in the morning , seeing the sun, I felt better.

***** ***** *****

Me and Dad- June 1988

Graduation from Middle Scho

My first visit to Mom -1987

Me in Bermuda

CHAPTER FOUR

Life feels quite different when you are told that finally you're going to belong to somebody. Poor original Mom and Dad, they gave birth to me, then died, like the red salmon who swim through fierce waters, giving birth, then dying. Mom wasn't really dead but with her cirrhosis, they had her permanently in a government hospital on Roosevelt Island. I hadn't seen her since she signed the papers allowing me to be adopted. We both knew it was the right thing. She couldn't care for me any more. Yes, I'd have a new family, a new home. Maybe a chance to be a better person. But I'd frown and tell God I wasn't such a bad person after all. What had I done that was so bad, to make the teachers (and that file) hate me so? Born with scars, born nonwhite, born into a disruptive family. . . maybe all that was bad, but I knew positively that Jesus considered me a good person, and I'd fight these biased white teachers and administrators (makers of THAT file) who would say otherwise of me. And, I made up my mind; I would not go into any new family who didn't fight for me, and people like me. Our rights.

As it so happened , Mr. Crowder (provided to us by Mrs. Butler of COAC) was everything I'd hoped he'd be. We met with Kathy at Little Flower's Brooklyn office. He had a good-looking face; he was smiling and I was smiling. As planned, we went to a nearby fast-food restaurant and ate a hamburger and french fries meal together. While light-brown in color, he had European features, nice hair, very warm eyes. He spoke like a news commentator on television; I soon realized he was a very smart man. He knew Spanish as well as I knew it, and he also spoke German, Italian, some Russian, Chinese, Tagalog, Japanese and Thai. He told me about his interesting work all those years he had been a Far East specialist with the United Nations. Now he was active rebuilding his houses and playing music as an organist in churches (he had been a member of the American Guild of Organists for more than forty years). He made life seem easy and I felt very comfortable with him. He had told the agency he wanted someone honest, who was

46

free of crime and drug problems. He knew that I was not involved in either, and the social worker had told him I was honest. This day we didn't talk about serious things, but I soon told him a few things about my life. The good things. Next, it was planned that I be brought into town every other weekend, and go out to his main house, to spend the weekends with him. His Flushing home was like a small International House, with foreign students. He had been taking them in for more than twenty years. He lived mostly in his huge stucco house just north of Yonkers, high up in the mountains, with a beautiful view of the Palisades in New Jersey as well as of the Hudson River.

It was a glorious house with piano, organ, stereo, huge Kutani and Imari vases, Chinese and Korean scrolls, Indian art and many paintings. He gave me a big bedroom to call my own, some games, a gold chain and a watch. Mrs. Bivona, the foster lady, kept telling me I was making a big mistake, and she'd take away the things 'that black man' gave me. One weekend in February 1987, she 'forgot' to pick me up where the bus left me in Long Island on my return. I had to sleep on the floor in the children's center. It was zero degrees outside! Mr. Crowder was so concerned that I didn't get home and call him. Once before he had telephoned home and Mrs. Bivona hit the ceiling, telling the agency he was never to call her house again. Well, this time he just waited it out and found out from the social worker that I was okay. He did write the agency, concerned that I had rattling in my chest. He insisted that they put me through exams, particularly for tuberculosis. Next, he bought me warmer clothing and I began to take better care of my own health.

I was very happy seeing Mr. Crowder that spring of 1987. One early thing he did was to arrange for me to visit my mother at her hospital. I hadn't seen Mom in a long time. We brought her flowers, and together we took photos with her and her Filipino nurses. She liked Mr. Crowder very much and thought he would make a good father for me. When June came around and school was over, Kathy came to get me and I packed all my things and said good-bye to Mrs. Bivona. I was going now to live with Mr. Crowder in the trial period before formal adoption. He had been urging Kathy to get me a passport as it was his custom to go abroad each year. Well, there were problems with that so we went instead to Cape Cod, followed by a trip west to California. Weilin Wang, from China, came with us, motoring to Massachusetts. Mr. Crowder's friends in Mashpee were all part-Indian, i.e., American Indian. We stayed with Viola Holtzclaw who owned a number of guest houses. I saw the Wigwam Motel which Mr. Crowder's uncle, Sol (who owned bars, a liquor store and hotel in Harlem) was to buy. Mr. Crowder himself was thinking about a house, but he hated driving so far. We did drive to Provincetown, and I enjoyed the sights very much. Next, we were at the beach; we saw the Kennedy compound, then off to Plymouth to see where the pilgrims landed, and the Mayflower. Coming home we stopped in Newport to see the millionaire cottages, as Mr. Crowder knew I liked big houses. Boy, I'd have lots to tell my classmates!

Going to California in August, it was my first time in an airplane. I was brave; I got used to the bathroom; coming down , the pain in my ears soon subsided. Once there, out West, I had more fun than I've ever had before!

One thing about Mr. Crowder, he was a man of high culture and had very good friends everywhere. In San Francisco we stayed with Dr. Ruth Howard in her beautiful home on Twin Peaks. Her father had been the bishop of the Episcopal church in Washington, D.C., and she and Mr. Crowder had been friends for more than thirty years. It was my first time being in the home of Negro people who were as white as whites. It made me realize that racial divisions are rather false. San Francisco was a city of great beauty. I enjoyed seeing Golden Gate Bridge (walking across it), Alcatraz and North Beach, riding the cable cars, shopping in Chinatown and in the Mission district, where we also visited an old Spanish church. Dr. Isa Huntington, an old friend of his from United Nations, came up on a bus from San Jose, and we had a delightful meal at the fancy St. Francis Hotel. Then, we went to two grand museums with her. She was past eighty and still full of life. She knew so many things (and she liked me). I wish I had had teachers like Dr. Huntington.

That evening I got very sick with an asthma attack. I thought I was going to die. I could not breathe. Dr. Howard and Mr. Crowder helped me to relax , then everything was all right. It may have been from the fancy lobster and clams we had at lunch, or from getting home at dusk in a thick San Francisco fog. Anyway, I was okay the next day and we enjoyed it by having another fancy dinner at a culinary club, as guests of Dr. Howard. Diane Marienthal (who used to be Dr. Bunche's secretary at United Nations) also drove up from San Jose to meet us. We met her new husband, John. A Japanese businessman, Mr. Aoki, came over from Berkeley to see my father-to-be and brought us a nice gift (a photograph album covered in Japanese silk). I didn't tell you but another one of Mr. Crowder's good friends from United Nations days came all the way from Tennessee to New York to join us on our trip to California. It was a nice Chinese lady from HongKong named Rae Neblett. She had been a war bride. Her American husband had just died and she was thinking about resettling in California. We had a lot of fun with Aunt Rae; she enjoyed eating Chinese food in different places. She also had relatives in the Bay Area.

Next, we took a bus to Monterey, Carmel and San Luis Obispo. In Monterey I enjoyed their new aquarium, and seeing the Pebble Beach golf club. We had ice cream in Carmel. In San Luis Obispo there was merely the Catholic church which was delightfully Spanish. Dad wanted me to see San Simeon but the bus went direct to Los Angeles. We got off right in Hollywood where our hotel was. My father-to-be mainly wanted to see an old army friend of his, Curtis Tann, an artist, who had just had a stroke. We got ourselves out to Altadena by bus and had a long walk (in hot desert sun) to the point where Tann's wife, Ethel, was to meet us. We rested several times to avoid heat stroke. But it was wonderful meeting his army friends. And they were nice to me. Down in Los Angeles we were to visit Judith Headlee-Still, the daughter of the famous Negro composer, William Grant Still. Here again was a whole family of people so completely white that you would not know that they were colored.

Judy took us to the museum which the City of Los Angeles had just established in the name of her father. We also went to Disneyland, and Knott's Berry Farm. It was the most fun I had had in years. Judy was so nice in driving us to many places including a movie star wax museum where I posed with Burt Reynold's look-alike. In our photo you'd think he was the real movie star. Down in Beverly Hills I saw Elvis Presley's house, and fancy Rodeo Drive. Before going down to Orange County to Judy's house my father-to-be and I spent three days in the penthouse suite in the fancy Roosevelt Hotel which used to be frequented by movie stars. (I could feel their ghosts there!) They had a magnificent outdoor swimming pool which I enjoyed. Mr. Crowder had stayed there before; now it was full of German tourists. His friend, Leo Branton, a lawyer, came to greet us. Later Mr. Crowder explained to me that Mr. Branton (who had also been an army friend) had represented Angela Davis in the famous trial in which she won, and also that his brother, Wiley, was the famous Arkansas lawyer who led the civil rights suit against Governor Faubus that opened the public schools to Negroes. Mr. Branton was fair-skinned, good-looking and very businesslike. While they were talking I was allowed to roam around. I found Hollywood Blvd. crazy; people were roller skating down the street at midnight! My father-to-be's niece, Angela Strachan, came to the hotel late one evening to visit us. She was a very pretty girl, and she liked me. Also, she was as white as any white person.

I remember now how Mrs. Bivona thought of Mr. Crowder as 'black', and how she'd make a big sneer whenever I returned from my visits with him. When she stole the gifts he had given me (a watch and gold chain) her spiteful act made me respect her no longer. She was a rather uneducated kind of Spanish who thought themselves nearly white and better than any Blacks. On the one hand, she hated to lose me for the money in it, and on the other hand, she hated to see a Spanish child go to a black man. Well, racial lessons we all must learn, including teachers and foster care people! I'd not follow what they were putting before me as 'good sense'. But I must tell you, I loved these new Americans I was meeting outside of New York, the colored, the near-white and the white. They all seemed closer together than people in the East. More alike! Or, maybe more American!

Another time Mr. Crowder took me to Michigan to meet his family in Detroit. I met his favorite cousin, Lawrence Higgins, who told me some of the family's history. He was a relative on his mother's side (the brown family), and they were rich too. Lawrence showed me pictures of their big houses in Georgia. Dr. P.S.L. Hutchins , their grandfather, came from a Free Negro family who owned a plantation, and as far back as the 1870s they sent their kids north to famous schools like Yale, Oberlin and Harvard for a proper education. Dr. Hutchins became a preacher and built five churches; he was also one of the founders and regents of Selma University in Alabama. I enjoyed hearing these stories about respectable people in the Afro-American community. I met other lovely people who had been old friends from Mr. Crowder's boyhood in Michigan during the Great Depression. He showed me the grammar school where he had gone. In those days it had only five colored kids. As he was very smart, he was double-promoted several times and finished the twelfth grade at sixteen. Yet, he said his immediate family in Detroit were rather poor in spite of their high culture. His near-white father had pioneered in coming north in the early 1920s, getting out on his own from his wealthy mixed family in Georgia. Detroit in those days was the greatest industrial city in the world. It prospered building all the motor cars , and it had excellent schools. But when the banks and Wall Street collapsed, his father was out of work for four years. And he was too proud to ask for money from his rich and blond Scotch-Irish father in Georgia. Mr. Crowder graduated from high school with honors, then he left home at age sixteen to put himself through the University of Michigan. Detroit people were proud of him for what he had accomplished alone and without family help. His cousin, Lawrence, drove by the family house Mr. Crowder as a newsboy had given his family the down payment money to buy. Next Lawrence showed me Motown, and told me how Mr.Crowder had been the first nonwhite to play with the Detroit Symphony, when in 1938 they used him to beef up the viola section for a memorial concert they gave for Ossip Grabrilowitz, their former conductor. Other than being one of the first blacks to sit on the stage at Orchestra Hall, he played NEA conventions at Statler and Book-Cadillac hotels (then with 'no blacks' policy). Also as a smart high school senior he was featured pianist in the school system's weekly radio programs on WWJ, WJR, WXYZ. While still a teenager, he had been a pioneer in many musical activities in old Detroit.

I liked Detroit, its beautiful churches and its very stable colored community. I felt sad that whites had all run away from this vibrant historical town. I particularly liked the clean Detroit River with its view of Windsor, Ontario. And Belle Isle with its zoo, its canal and Aquarium. Mr. Crowder showed me pictures he had taken there back in the 1930s. He was handsome then, and looked white! (Mr. Crowder told me to take this out, that he likes being 'black'. No, he hates that word 'black', saying there was nothing wrong with 'Negro'. He says: whites did this; changed the naming of a whole race! He agreed with his friend, the late Roy Wilkins, head of the NAACP, seeing nothing in this new 'blackness' business.) We went sightseeing in his old neighborhood near Indian Village (still very very nice) with his old friends, the Louis Proctors. Therapist Suesetta McCrae took us to dinner at a soul food place. It was great food! Downtown near our hotel in Renaissance Center I was introduced to Congressman John Conyers, and I took a ride on the People Mover (sightseeing train) which passed the Joe Louis Arena and through old Greek town, right next to new modern apartments Negroes were building.

Next we went to Canada and the border guards wanted to see papers on me because they thought I was a runaway Mexican trying to get into Canada. Lastly, we had dinner with one of his old friends, Roberta and Bob Fuller, a dentist. (I enjoyed meeting their two very nice teenage daughters, Jennifer and Pamela). I met Dr. Bob's mother who at age 93 was still active. She played the piano for me, and told me that I was handsome. Mrs. Fuller was related to the Lewis & Clark Expedition's leader. Our teachers never teach that people of color are so a part of America's history. They really don't have to because these good people, just as fair-skinned as whites and proud of their Afro-American roots, basically think of themselves as being American first, and certainly as such they would make known their families' roles in history other than the drab stories most teachers tell, associating colored people only with slavery. I was planning to tell my class at school about Mr. Crowder's great-great grandfather being appointed by President Andrew Johnson as provincial governor of Georgia in 1865, and about his uncle, Joseph Clark, who was President Eisenhower's assistant postmaster-general. Mr. Crowder said teachers would not want to hear that.

All of this strangely began to make me feel better about myself. I was joining somebody who was richly American and would fight for me to also join the world in a good place in spite of whites trying to edge me out. The real spooky part of my life was that whites were still in control of me. I could not advance at school without their consent. Mr. Crowder told the Proctors some things about my problems, and we looked at a nice private art school in Detroit where I might go. He felt and they felt that in Michigan I certainly would not face the racism I was facing in New York schools. On my way home I thought again about my problems. Yes, I knew I was a little lazy in school, but I had NEVER A WORD OF ENCOURAGEMENT. Yes, they judged me harshly while eating all the fish and bread, giving me nothing.

Now, taking all these trips with Mr. Crowder, I felt like I was learning important things. Why couldn't education be based on exposure to life in real terms? And my hopes for improving myself in life went up. In New York, in driving between his two houses, Mr. Crowder often picked up from two to four ladies he knew at the United Nations, who lived in Queens. Mrs. LaBhar from Morocco, Mrs. Ferraro from Belgium, Mrs. Salgado from Haiti and Mrs. Bazarra from Egypt.They all liked me and talked to me. But while in the car, they all were speaking French! I would listen and soon I knew a few words of French, and would answer their greetings in French. It made me feel very proud of myself. (But at school I would be given no credit for having any language ability!) Now I've made myself work much harder, not to please school teachers but to please him. Also, I want to prove to myself my good qualities, while satisfying his expectations of me. Some nasty teachers told him he was pushing me too hard. I never felt that. I've only wished they were as honest and as helpful as Mr. Crowder! He'd **never** mark me down as they've been doing to me. He merely wants me to get the best of myself, develop it, and to be ready (as he says) to take up an honorable place in MY GENERATION OF AMERICA.I've moved in this direction, nobly I believe, but I still don't understand why I must work so hard at school when **none** of them give me any credit for being capable!

Mr. Crowder does pounce on me at home for not picking up my clothes and things. I drink a lot of soda and leave glasses and pop bottles everywhere. (Now this house has no Rebecca to clean up after me; she's passed on.) He says order in living is a must. Also he makes me put the cap on the toothpaste. (But our house, during the writing period of this book, became hopelessly cluttered with papers. Some of them papers for my future.) Mr. Crowder thinks I've become too used to others providing for me, that I'm not prepared if I ever really had a thirsty or hungry day. I've tried to develop that get-up-and-go spirit, but it's hard for me, first with the schooling mess, and secondly, I am a bit weak physically. And my self esteem has been damaged, when teachers took and still take all my good efforts and crush them, giving me nothing. So injured, I enjoy relaxing , doing nothing at times. I don't think I could live without my relaxing moments. I don't tell Mr. Crowder that my fighting spirit still is not aroused, but I think he knows it because he does get disturbed when he sees that I don't wear the eyeglasses he's bought me, and I go to bed without setting my alarm clock. And it hurts him to see tears in my eyes when I arrive home from school. Those are injustice tears, he says, not tears of feeling sorry for myself. To him I've grown tremendously. My IQ is up 30%, but try convincing teachers of this! He tells me one must take injustice tears and make a fight of it. Now about the alarm clock, he says I must always look to tomorrow, and greet each new day with enthusiasm!

*****   *****   *****

CHAPTER FIVE

In the spring of 1987 while I was still a ward of Little Flower, and visiting Mr. Crowder on weekends, we made our formal visit to the school in his town. Kathy Pearson came with us to explain that I'd be going to their middle school in September, and she was now ready to turn over the "File". Nobody smiled and nobody said 'welcome' to me, the new student. I soon heard them telling Kathy how much money they wanted from the other school district where I had been in attendance. Mr. Crowder looked at me, confused. He had for years been paying a whopping $4,000 a year for local school tax, and he was retired and had no children in this school. Over $40,000 he had paid, and they wouldn't even say 'good morning' to him. One of the officials at the meeting made it clear that school here for me would probably be difficult because , they said, their children were two years *above* national average. **NOBODY TALKED AS IF I HAD A RIGHT TO BE AT THIS SCHOOL,** to progress at my own speed. Mr. Sobet, the psychologist, did smile at me at the end of the meeting, and he told me he'd be around that summer if I wanted to come in and 'talk'. The ladies in the group (a teacher, an administrator, a guidance counselor) were all serious business (looking like hags). Rather nasty towards me, I felt. But I knew I had to put such thoughts out of my head. Yes, this was a new start. While they had no inclination to look at me squarely, or to say anything nice to me, these were my teachers I had to respect.

That summer Mr. Crowder was very busy with architects and builders. He had decided to add three rooms to the second floor of his country house, to give me space for myself and for my mother to visit occasionally. Making it an eleven-room house would be a costly job, and he explained to me how he had planned the financing of it. He would sell off his CDs for me! He said that some day it would be my own house, and I was glad to hear that. He claimed that I would always find peace in that house, and I believed him.

We finally hired a jovial, big-stomach, tough-looking Italian contractor, and the ripping-down work began that November 1987. They had to take off the existing front roof, the nice little crescent windows, everything but the massive facade of pinkish-yellow stones that was the beauty of this well-built house. The same pinkish-yellow stones skirted the basement level, and were in the living room's giant fireplace. Once the roof was off, we took pictures of me standing in the void which would be my own private bedroom. It gave me a good secure feeling.

Every day there were six or eight workmen at the house when I came home from school. I think I was doing okay at Hastings Middle School. My teacher was a nice black lady, Miss Tibbs. And I adored my principal, Miss Stalma. But the peace and calm wasn't to last. They had given me a speech teacher, Mrs. Krim (not really full-time), and I was to fit her into my schedule somehow. They had me going to her house for my lessons. She lived near the school. Her husband was paraplegic (I had to look this word up.). Well, Mrs. Krim kept changing the schedule. Some times she wanted to see me Tuesdays at three, then Fridays at two. "Oh," she'd say, "And next week I won't be available." Well, it became difficult for me to keep up with all these changes. My father-to-be told me to write it down in a notebook. I did, then I'd forget to read my notebook. Soon my father-to-be was amazed to get home a formal note that I had missed some sessions with Mrs. Krim, and would be given demerits for this. I felt sickened. I had tried my very best, and if I missed any after-school speech classes, maybe it was once or twice. We discussed the problem. I told Mr. Crowder that once when I went, on schedule, Mrs. Krim wasn't even there! So the blame should not be only on me. He smiled, tapping my knee and saying everything would be all right. But everything was not all right. These suburban white people were blaming me, and putting bad things in my record, and I wanted to have a good record. Always.

Yes, the serious part of our discussion had to deal with negative reports. Dad knew that I had taken Mrs. Krim for a friend and that I was very disappointed that she would turn in a report on me like this, and without any discussion with me. Also there was an administrator walking the halls who always stared at me as if I were one of the bad black boys from Graham-Windam. One day he approached me and asked me where was I going. Merely to the bathroom! He turned in a report on me, saying I was loitering in the halls. When Mr. Crowder and I discussed it I told him that I was merely going to the bathroom, and he believed me. White teachers don't believe you! When I write this I want you to realize that there is a first burden of race on all nonwhite children in suburban schools, and a second burden if they are learning disabled. A smart colored kid might slide by, but usually the suspicion and knifing is there. They make things tougher for you. I began to see this; many things were not as nice as my school days in the Ghetto.

Their punishing me so much felt like 'double jeopardy'. Mr. Crowder, comforting, said I merely had to work harder, and always keep my mind on business, on appearances. Then he explained quietly that any brown-faced boy, new in town, in _This Town_ could be looked upon as someone making trouble. He said: keep my good side shining; bring apples to my teachers. Soon they'd know me as someone of good reputation. But I'm very quiet. I don't push out, and I don't defend myself. Yes, he said, we all should speak up when we know we are in the right. But he warned me to stay clear of that blond administrator. Rules had to be obeyed.

In this whole town if you went to the A & P , the video shop, or the school, people were always watching you, because, the only colored youth in the town were bad boys (they said). Actually any dark-skinned boys in town were likely to be in foster care at the three millionaire estates which had turned into homes for children without families. These kids were not 'belongers' in town; most of them were brought in from New York City. The Bronx. Most whites looking at me thought I was a Graham-Windam or Children's Village kid just because I wasn't white!! And equally some thought I was delinquent, and thus all the demerits. Well, not exactly. At school, they knew Mr. Crowder was rich and lived in the good section of town. With their kooky minds, that could be a reason why they marked me down. Several times when I was walking home, cops would stop me and ask me where I was going. When I'd say "I live just there", they wouldn't believe me. Once they went ringing the doorbell to see if Dad was home. They'd never do that to a Jewish kid in town.

In early December, we went with Amelia Charles to Christmas Village, Pa. with a busload from UN. We had Christmas with Mark and Elizabeth Wehle. Work on the house had stopped after the new Anderson windows were put in. Now the outside wall was black tarpaper. They'd wait till spring to put on the new stucco. And all winter their big ladders would be standing straight up against the house. Once the wind blew a heavy ladder lopsided. I had to help Mr. Crowder straighten it up again. When the snows came, we went to Orlando, Florida for our vacation. I really enjoyed Disneyworld as much as I had Disneyland in California. We met a nice Scottish couple who were tourists too. They always spoke nicely to us. When the van came each morning to our hotel to pick us up to take us to Epcot Center or Disneyworld, my father and I said 'good morning' to the people already on the bus. Nobody would speak. But, when any white persons got on, they all said 'good morning' to them.

That spring, the Italian man doing our house had his West Indian workers back at our place. They came taking my father's aspirins, his tools, his radios, his anti-freeze. Yes, they were always looking for freebies, and they got good salaries. The Italian man made Mr. Crowder go to the bank each week to get him big money, so he could "meet his payroll", he would say. Often when it rained, nobody came to work on the house, still, the Italian man would come on Friday to get his money. Dad went so often to the bank the lady teller there thought he was under attack by some scam team. Half of this was true! Many things were broken in the house: the mirrors, a beautiful large alabaster statue that had graced our foyer. The faucets in the basement where they washed up. Cigarette burns on our good Oriental carpets. When Mr. Crowder would approach the Italian about all this, he'd merely laugh and would say: "Don't worry; I'm gonna get you new carpets!"

Most of the work on the house was completed in the spring of 1988, and I enjoyed having my two new rooms all to myself. They had been made with twelve-foot slanting ceilings, made of beautiful wood which matched the original wood ceiling of the porchroom downstairs. And we'd have gorgeous ceiling fans hanging in the new rooms. When the old town-electrician came to do his work, hanging the fans, he'd scream at my father as if he were a slave. When he saw 'Made in Taiwan' on one fan, he yelled "Take it back!" And Mr. Crowder drove the forty miles in zero weather. They tested it, saying it was okay. When he brought it back, now the electrician hung it without further ado. Mr. Crowder was angry that evening. A racist white man had tested him, would boss, and charge big money for it. The electrician's bill was $4,000, just for wiring three rooms, hanging fans and putting in a new fuse box in the basement. A neighbor laughed, saying you could wire a whole new house for that price.

Originally when the work began that last November they had two four-man teams tearing down the house: one white and one Negro. When the inside work began, one Negro man was put in charge. The white workers complained. The Italian had put the man in charge who was the only graduate carpenter, and had the most experience. The white guys didn't like this and the two groups argued so, the Italian boss soon took the white team off the job. Well, as times were bad and they didn't have another job to go to, the white guys were mad. One of them, Tony, went out and got drunk, then at midnight he called us, saying he was coming to burn the house down. He also told some stories on the Italian bossing the job. Mr. Crowder, just sighing, never thought he would be in the middle of a labor dispute. But it cautioned him not to be too sure his Italian leader was an honest man. He soon briefed his lawyer about this job, in case more serious troubles might come.

In February Mr. Crowder had to go to Milwaukee for a television interview covering a new book he had written on the Civil War. I was confident I could take care of myself in his absence, but there were workers all over the house, so I did not feel alone. As the new rooms finally got finished I found myself relaxing downstairs rather than upstairs which had been built expressly for me. Actually I did start out upstairs in my new rooms. A big paper-mache loinhead had been put in the hallway by my bedroom. It was super, with big red tongue and snarling teeth. I played Nintendo in my new bedroom, but the next door neighbor came ringing the bell, complaining that I was too noisy and I disturbed his sleeping baby. Well, I went downstairs again, sleeping there, and was soon never in the new rooms built for me. The morning room had been a former guest bedroom. It was very sunny in mornings, and I liked its Victorian look, its cartouches and friezes. Its art objects, paintings from China or Japan, made me feel as if I were in the Orient. Mr. Crowder put cable television in that room, just for me, and a new color TV set. I liked it so well I decided to sleep there. Mr. Crowder slept on the second floor in the master suite. So I really had the downstairs all to myself, and I did all my lessons there. I had a perfect environment, and there was absolutely no reason why, with my good mind, (*listen teachers!*) I couldn't become a super student there.

Yes, we did have a lot of trouble with that contractor, overcharging, stealing, and walking off the job. Mr. Crowder always kept me involved in money matters, as he felt this was a way of strengthening me in mathematics. I was allowed to have both a checking and a savings account, and when I told this at school, teachers acted jealous. Our house, I learned, had been built by Hollywood people, a lawyer for movie stars. They had another big house in Forest Hills Gardens, and one in Beverly Hills. (They brought two sequoia trees from Hollywood and they are still on our lawn.) Their niece, Pat Holly, who had been our next door neighbor, sold her house and moved to North Carolina. Her family had been on the block since 1912 when the Hudson Heights area was settled by Norwegians. Then when Billie Burke, Flo Ziegfeld and other Hollywood people came to town, a tennis club and a boating club rose up at river's edge, but mainly this town's riverfront was covered with big ugly factories. The main one until 1975 was Anaconda. Now all the factories are gone. This town of merely 9,000 had taxed them so heavily, they all left! Now, the town looks dilapidated with the movie stars gone, Anaconda gone, and the other factories gone. Now the big taxes have to come solely from the home owners. They had thought they could attract a Japanese firm or two, but it never happened. Then in recent years, some Bronx types came to our town, with all their prejudice, or, their over-pride at being white and in the yuppie circuit. I've heard that six Nobel Prize winners have lived in the town, but I personally, do not like it very much. People are not friendly. They like to be stiff-necked, and "more important than you". One of our friends told us that all American suburban bedroom towns have people with similar personalities, wrapped up in their new status.

On the other side of our house our neighbor had been Judge Edward Brancati. He and his wife, Helen, had been very friendly with Mr. Crowder before I came. But Judge Brancati died and his wife sold the house and moved to Florida. With the taxes being very high , many good people have sold out and moved away. The new neighbors became young people, rarely needing to be friendly as they had friends of their own. And some are upset if they see an Afro-American anywhere near them. They'll try to dictate to you, as the new white-American young generation often does to People-of-Color. Mr. Crowder, who writes, has always thought of himself as American first. I can't quite think that way the way they push me around at school. He says we should avoid having angry words with people. Once in a while he has to scold me for doing wrong things. Mostly I get into trouble for lying. I guess it's a security factor from days when I was alone and had to protect myself. Nevertheless, we get along very nicely together. And if there is icy behavior around us, we ignore it, trying to pay more attention to our secure little world-of-learning. When the local paper wrote a story on Mr. Crowder , some people sneered at someone thinking himself both white and colored. They don't want to know that history that includes good black people. Mr. Crowder has traveled so much, he is more comfortable in other places, I know, but he says he'll stick it out until I finish my education. We're both internal people, and we enjoy our abode to ourselves. And mine was a perfect setup for a boy growing into his teen years and one wanting privacy and a place of his own, where he could study and learn things.

You'd like Mr. Crowder. He was always thinking of me, my needs, my desires. I became rather worried, being around these whites who think they are better than we are. I'd like to tell him to send me to school in town, New York City, but I'm even afraid there. I don't like bad boys. Knowing my desires for learning, that spring Mr. Crowder found me a tutor in art. Debbie was good and I learned a lot, but she was dating and couldn't give me much time.

On Easter Sunday we took Mom into the City for church, and attended services at both St. Patrick's and St. Thomas' on Fifth Avenue. She enjoyed seeing the Easter Parade. Upon leaving quiet Roosevelt Island after taking her back, we had a car accident. As we exited from a deserted parking lot, turning into the main road , a Filipino rushing away from his job just minutes before three, saw us in the intersection, but he couldn't wait. As he tried to squeeze past us at fast speed, he swerved in the narrow lane, scraping his car against ours. He was going to rush on but Mr. Crowder signaled him to stop and see the damage. No damage was done to us, but there was a long gash in the side of the man's van. Now he was mad and quick to blame us. He got other Filipinos, just leaving their hospital jobs , to support him saying we caused the accident. They weren't even there! Well, Mr. Crowder was relieved when the cops finally came. Most disturbing, our insurance company for years accepted the Filipino's view. Some technicality about the person on the main road always being right, and one turning into the main road, always wrong. In his knowledge of law Mr. Crowder felt Americans were too apt to generalize, and I remembered this when later I had trouble in college. And, by all means, majority opinion could hurt innocent men, even me in my schooling! We paid the higher premiums and went on with life.

Mr. Crowder is a friendly man with no real racial feelings. He regards people as colorless, *all the same,* and that's the way he wants me to think. In May his good friend, Mr. Lesch, visited us from

Indiana with his teenage boy from Puerto Rico. Robert lives with his mother in San Juan. It had been an interracial marriage, and Robert, while blond like his father, taught me a certain nonchalance about Puerto Ricans. His father had been a New York probation officer, and he could be tough. Mr. Crowder needed a little sympathy about the botched-up expensive renovation job. His friend was a little too quiet, not really understanding how we had had racial pressures in the renovation job. Robert and I talked about lighter things.

I sort of had a girlfriend, a nice Indian girl I had met in middle school. Her father was in the diplomatic corps of some Latin country where there were East Indians and Negroes. The mother had a West Indian maid she treated much like a slave. I was allowed to go Sundays to visit with my friend and her family at their nice home in the rich area of Scarsdale. That spring I had also joined Hastings' Troop No. 2 of the Boy Scouts of America. In that group I made a few friends. We'd meet weekly at the Reformed Church. Guys in my platoon would telephone me at home when we had chores to do such as selling Christmas wreaths or selling tickets out in front of the A & P. When there was a big wrestling match on cable television, Mr. Crowder let me invite in a dozen guys, and we had a party. I also went on field trips with Kevin and a few others I liked.

My other pleasure was movies. I liked horror films mostly. I was allowed to go to the mall on Central Park Avenue, to see films on Sundays. I'd walk the two miles home on a beautiful country road called Jackson Avenue. Often local whites would race by in their cars, shouting obscenities at me ("Go back where you came from!") Some tried to run me down on that road, and again, cops would stop me and ask where was I going. Once in a while Mr. Crowder would drive me over in his nice shiny Chevrolet car, and we'd see a film together. I remember we saw Good Mornin', Vietnam , and , Stand and Deliver, the latter about Spanish kids trying to get a decent education in Los Angeles. Mr. Crowder also took me and his friend, Odella, down to New York City to see Broadway shows. I saw several off-Broadway dramas, and a fantastic Rock show from Russia. The live music was superb. Also I enjoyed a small German company in a sort of political satire musical.

After several school meetings on me, that spring, I finally graduated from middle school that June of 1988. For the evening ceremony Dad and I dressed carefully and went to the school's auditorium for the ceremony. By the end of the first half hour it all became boring because they were calling the same names of kids to get all the awards. While we all (including special education kids) were listed in the program in alphabetical order, when they called us up to get our diplomas, we six special ed kids were put at the very end of the line. They made us the very LAST , as a group, to go up on stage and get our diplomas. No more alphabetical order, we were just last, as if we were the inferior ass-end of everything! Dad and I left that place feeling very depressed. When I got home I broke out in tears. Mr. Crowder comforted me because he knew that the one thing we wanted was TO BELONG. . .to be intermeshed with the other kids, to be accepted as normal, and not isolated and put *at the end* like this. He complained to the School Board and they listened icily to his complaints and said meekly that they wouldn't let it happen again.

That spring we were still getting inspected by the Little Flower Children's Services. Mr. Crowder had filed for a second child, being that he was so old, he wanted me to have a brother and lifelong friend, after his death. He had to go through the home study, the house viewing and get another medical, and fill in a lot of papers, but after all that, we didn't get any offers from them.

That April I was told at school that I could not go to high school in town. They claimed they had no facilities for special education students in their high school. I'd have to be bussed to another town. They gave my father-to-be a choice of two schools: Greenburgh and Rye Neck. Mr. Crowder was to visit both schools. When he went to Greenburgh with the nice Miss Wilma Gilbert, the BOCES lady, he was surprised to find something like a ghetto school, overloaded with unruly blacks. Certainly there were white people in the neighborhood but only few sent their children to this particular school. The fact that they only gave me two choices was somewhat mysterious, he thought. He knew that Westchester County had plenty of excellent schools, and now that his school taxes had gone up to $4,300, he wanted to make sure that we'd get our money's worth, a good school where I could learn.

Rye Neck was distant from our house, almost twenty miles, but it was the better school and we chose it. That would mean almost three hours of bus-riding a day, because, in this new setup, I had to be bussed to still another school in the mornings. I'd have to take vocational subjects at BOCES , Grasslands, Valhalla, each and every morning. (They first gave me a choice of flower decorating or

62

auto mechanics. My subjects to study! My father was amazed, because he knew that I had many more suitable aptitudes. He complained, but the system did not promise me anything sane or logical. Some school people would make decisions in their usual way, and this could waste your life if you did not complain.)

That summer, I went to Boy Scout camp. When I got back I got an early birthday present of a set of encyclopedia. Next, Mr. Crowder decided, to get away from it all, we'd take a cruise to Bermuda. We left on Saturday, July 16th on the Queen of Bermuda. Mr. Crowder had sailed with them before on a trip to Mexico, so he knew several in the crew including the captain. He had arranged a birthday celebration for me as soon as we were out of port. In the great dining hall, with birthday cake, candle, and mariachi band . When everybody asked me to name a song, I named *La Bamba,* and of course they all sang *Happy Birthday* to me. It was a lively ship with fantastic shows. I met the comic, Larry Larkin, and bought one of his tapes. And I enjoyed myself hanging out at the pool and the disco. I had my own charge card and I bought a nice necklace souvenir for my mom. I found a very expensive watch, and turned it in; the old man to whom it belonged said he was going to give me a reward, but he never did. In Hamilton, Mr. Crowder asked me if I wanted to rent a motor scouter, but I said no. Instead, we went to an evening parade in the town square, with a white man dressed in top hat performing as town-crier, and natives dancing around in real African fashion. Next, we took an expensive taxi ride out to an underground cave , saw the churches, and finally went to fancy Elbow Beach. Back on the ocean, the water was rough at night, and I was allowed to roam around and think of myself as a pirate or ancient sea captain. It was fun!

In September the yellow bus came to our house each morning for me. Up early and home late. Since they had me half time in vocational studies at Valhalla, Dad wanted to make sure that the studies were useful to me. But the hardheaded teaching people still had me in auto mechanics! When I came home one day and told him they had me in a welding class, with goggles, he hit the ceiling. He asked them didn't they understand that I only had ONE GOOD EYE? They shrugged shoulders and tried to defend their stupidness. Dad insisted I be allowed to try office skills. They hesitated; it was like they were giving away a piece of gold. Finally, they relented and I was allowed to have an interesting class in office skills.

In the afternoons another bus would take me from Valhalla to Rye Neck where I would have two hours of academic work. (Only two hours!) Very often the morning bus would fail to pick me up at home. Dad would frantically have to call the bus people in Dobbs Ferry. The schools took no direct interest, and several times he had to stop what he was doing and drive me the twenty miles to school. My father claimed that this setup did not allow me to get a proper education. A bus system needed to be under direct school control. He had told them many times that arrangements were not logical. He did not like my three hours a day of riding on busses. Whenever the weather changed: rain, fog or snow, there'd be no bus on time. Very often after weekends my bus driver wouldn't show up for work (maybe drunk), and they'd forget about me until we made our frantic phone calls. I'd get to my classes late. And if I miss something in learning, merely a negative report would be written up on me, and never any mention of a bus problem.

On normal days, I 'd leave home around seven in the mornings, getting home shortly after four. Dad would be looking at Phil Donahue whom he claimed was America's great racial mentor. I'd relax with my TV, looking at old cartoons. Soon, I'd go to my math tutor, Mrs. Kenny, who lived across the street from us. Then dinner and more study! After a while, the Special Ed teachers at Rye Neck High began picking on me, complaining that I did not do all my homework, or, that I forgot to turn something in. They'd call my father and speak abusively to him.(In my talking at school, I'd praise him and boast a bit, and they didn't like that.) Calmly my father would remind them of the reason I was in special education, one of my disabilities was forgetfulness, but he assured them that he would get me turning in lessons whenever he knew that they were due. They never advised him of anything; they preferred to give me a bad mark in their permanent papers. My father also explained to them that I was spending too much time on busses, and that all my free time was spent on schoolwork. They didn't believe him. From the jokes I heard among teachers they were a bit jealous about the fancy way we lived, all the trips we took and the important people we knew. So, they'd keep their concept: James Isn't Studying Hard Enough! And as one teacher said: "James will get no **free ride** at Rye Neck!"

***** ***** *****

64

(r. to l.) With Dr. Wang in Toronto; the Gehms in Northbrook; the Proctors in Detroit; Dr. Chen in Chicago - 1990

CHAPTER SIX

I was adopted by Mr. Crowder on 22 November 1988. It was front page news in the Gannett newspapers. The Dept. of Social Services had recommended that our story be told, and newspeople came to our house in advance to quiz us and to take many pictures of me and Dad, and even shots of me with Rosie, my cat. Mr. Crowder had cautioned them not to make it racial; they had promised this, but in the end, the story published was all racial! They talked about a successful multiracial man who could have adopted any color, but chose to take me, a minority Puerto Rican. The story wasn't true as to choices. The agencies with their extreme racial bias had always pushed for Mr. Crowder to get a ghetto child, black and nothing else. It was he who had insisted they recognize his mixed heritage, and that is how he got me. He told me that children technically listed as black-and-white usually went to white families, especially if they were fair enough to be taken for all-white. Then in his class sessions he had had to take before getting me, he said it sickened him to listen to white families who had taken mixed kids complain about not knowing how to handle them once they reached the dating age. And mixed families who were waiting for such children usually could not get them. White families had first pick of even the half-Negro kids.

I was a bit uncomfortable at school after all the newspaper publicity. Some laughing white guys in the hall called me 'white nigger'. The teachers didn't stop them. I told Dad and he told me to be strong and stand tall. He knew and I knew that Puerto Rican was the same mixture of Caucasian, Indian and Negro that Mr. Crowder had. While I had entered my new world ready to think 'black', Mr. Crowder told me I could stay middleground and be anything I wanted to be. Where the school forms asked for race, he told me to say 'other'. And I'd enter this new life not especially thinking color . But the teachers constantly thought of color, and when they tried to put me in a sleeve, I resisted. And I did not like their silly generalizations about Afro-Americans, nor the silly films we had to watch at school

66

about big city blacks. The stories were too racially defined, and exaggerations of the truth. Dad told me to stop talking so much about us in social studies because the more they knew, the more they were apt to penalize me for our lifestyle. The way they taught, poverty was generally the black man's fault, for not having enough get-up-and-go. Never was the white man blamed for any of the problems. And their talk about slavery was a farce. We had so many books in our home on the Civil War, I knew it backwards. No, I didn't discuss the truths we knew; it would shock them. Their talks always emphasized the secondary status of nonwhites; there was no growth for teacher or student, just the catechism they wanted us to learn.

My favorite teacher, Miss Bourland, was the arts teacher and she never challenged who I am. Earlier I had mentioned to my main teacher, Miss Trasda, all the important people Mr. Crowder knew. I also told her his great-great grandfather, James Johnson, had been briefly the governor of Georgia. Not believing a word of it, she said to me: "Yes, and I'm Madonna's sister." And when I brought from our home a silver tea service dating back to the 1850s and a copy of General Grant's letter to Robert E. Lee instructing him how to surrender his troops, (that was an April 1865 document, all yellow and crumbly), well, their mouths dropped open, wondering how we got such important papers. Still, this didn't help me any in my schooling. They, in fact, became doubly hard on me. I had to do everything near-perfect.

As usual that November we drove down to Jenkintown, Pennsylvania for Thanksgiving. My new father had for more than twenty years always spent Thanksgiving with his school friend, Paul Hensley, a Kentuckian, a Princeton grad, a Wall Street whiz, and a very loyal friend. He and his wife, Bettye, took me in as one of the family and I enjoyed being with them in their very luxurious home (right next door to the old Gimbel estate). We always had a good time with the Hensleys (very brainy people), and there was no reason to discuss 'race'. The one thing I did learn, there were Afro-Americans (still poor and humble) in this rich town, and Aunt Bettye said they had been there as long as the whites. This was Quaker country, full of history. But I was careful telling at school the new things I was learning about the Quakers. Once when I asked a teacher, Mrs. Goldstone, whether there were white slaves, she snapped back 'no'. But from reading our many history books and encyclopedia at home, I learned there certainly were white slaves, starting with the Jews in Egypt and right into the Middle East where the rich Arabs today are part-Negro. And in Russia there were white slaves (only, American whites call them 'serfs' and 'peons'). Dad says the idea of people making so much of Africans being slaves is a ploy in our modern times to keep the public thinking lowly of the Negro and his heritage. And, to keep us from getting things the others have.

That Christmas Dad gave me a Casio keyboard. I was so excited and proud of my gift that I cried. No one had ever remembered me like this. He hugged me and made me feel very welcome. We were at his Flushing house, to bring gifts to his tenants. Dad's favorite tenant, Weilin Wang, from China was given a nice warm blanket. His parents from Red China were also our guests (and I learned to speak a little Chinese with them). That Christmas Eve I offered the senior Mr. Wang some egg nog and he answered me in Chinese, a very definite 'yes'. The senior Wangs from South China had been put in jail for four years under the Mao regime, for being intellectuals. They stayed three months with us, and were always very gracious, trying to help out; they'd clean the lawn, neatly stacking up all the twigs. Once I went with them to the Statue of Liberty, and I got lost from them. Also Dad had taken them to the United Nations where they had a great visit. Weilin was about ready to get his doctor's degree in Computer Science. On Christmas day we drove to Scarsdale where Dad was the guest organist at the fancy Our Lady of Fatima Roman Catholic Church. We also had with us Antonio Salgado, a foster care kid from Children's Village. And in the end, I was allowed to spend time with my Mom, Carmen Puente, at her Roosevelt Island hospital, and with my grandmother, Esther Gonzalez, at her nice apartment in the Bronx.

Something very difficult for us happened that Christmas. Leaving Hastings, as we entered the highway, going to Queens, some white boys threw a huge rock at us, shattering the glass window where I sat. Dad came immediately off the highway to a gas station in Yonkers. He tried to call the police but the station owner didn't want him 'parking' his car unless he was going to buy gas. He saw we had an emergency, but he didn't care. On the next street, we met a nice Irishman who invited us into his home, while we waited for the police. When they came, and heard our story, they shrugged their shoulders and said they could do nothing because, even though we were in Yonkers, the highway is State property. They couldn't even look for the boys, they claimed. Soon a black cop from the State Troopers came. He was nice. The next day he called home and told us that several other people had been hit by stones at that same spot, but the Yonkers cops would do nothing. Yet, while they were there merely standing with us, one of them said he thought he knew who the boys were!

My mind was working overtime after that traumatic experience. The car window shattered just where I sat, by my right eye, my only good eye. Had glass entered my eye, I could have become completely blind. Yes, I think Jesus, or somebody in God's court, was watching over me, saving me, and assuring me that one day I would have a useful life.

As 1989 began, I was struck with a very heavy sinus cold. Mr. Crowder too (I now have to call him Dad). Our car began giving us trouble, and Dad was making plans to take me to some nice sunny place in the spring. He kept himself busy with our brand new LE computer. Some guy from the store was coming to our house giving lessons, at $50 an hour. The worst of it, the man seemed to be learning the computer himself; always sitting at it, not letting Dad write down routines he wanted to remember. My rigorous routine of study continued. Up at 6:30 and off to school at 7:15, getting home at five; a bit of television, then off to the tutor, then back to open my books and start writing my lessons. I was rather good in math because they let us use hand calculators.

My father told me I had to know math in my head, so as we drove along the highways, he'd drill me in multiplication tables and in division. He said my problems of memory had something to do with organization, fear and rejection. He wanted me sure of things, no matter the chastising of teachers. I began remembering various math routines, and stopped the guessing. I had been so alone in my early school years (without family) that I would panic at how to learn things, so I just started guessing, and this was a bad habit of mine. He got me reviewing things, closing my book and eyes, and thinking in my head, then talking aloud to see if I could remember textbook things just reviewed. Soon, I was remembering more! But when teachers discounted my work, I fell back to letting it be difficult for me to concentrate. Some things were boring, and underneath I was still worried about my mom and others of my real family. When I told Dad

I hated studying so long, he told me I was a lazy Puerto Rican used to getting things handed to him. Yes, his was racial joking but it did perk me up. And I knew his kind of joking was the real thoughts of some of my teachers.

When teachers continued to call Mr. Crowder saying I didn't have all my lessons done he soon complained to higher authorities, in my defense, saying I had too much homework for someone who spent three hours a day on the bus. Well, somebody behind the scenes did something, then they began getting me home at four o'clock! Inside I felt disappointed that my teachers never thought of all these problems I had. For them, I simply had to produce *exactly like the others!* I felt betrayed.

Some times Miss Trasda acted like a friend; other times she was mean as could be. She told my dad that if she pressured me, I'd do more work. He felt I was under too much pressure, and whenever I had asthma attacks he could trace it to matters happening at school. Soon Miss Trasda made a nuisance of herself calling him too many times with complaints about my work; then she started sending in written reports of delinquency for my file.(None of the other kids I knew in class got this.) Soon she was making Dad so mad, exaggerating my unpreparedness, that he stopped going to school meetings. He told them that he was old and that he couldn't drive the twenty miles in the snow, and that they should tell him on the telephone what was wrong or what needed to be improved. And he fought loyally for me whenever they wrote very bad reports to go to my file. They did compliment him on one thing: they told him they thought it was a nice thing he was doing, taking me on so many trips. But they still thought of me as someone from the Ghetto, someone with a retarded mind. He had me taking vitamins, especially vitamin C, and I could feel a new surge of energy. Now Mr. Crowder had told me: I simply was not retarded, that I had a good mind, that my files were wrong. He was often amazed at my intelligence, and I had an uncanny memory for directions; I could guide him to places where we had only been once. This meant, he said, that I should be doing good in school, if those silly people would forget what was in my files. He said I merely had to work on my laziness, (which was baggage from my previous life). Some laziness, he said was excusable as he himself had been that way in growing teen years as one approaches manhood. He'd rather I be that than doing sinful things in the streets! Teachers don't think that way. For them, you have to be near-perfect.

Teachers were never concerned with what I had been through. When I did very well at some school work, they took the credit when credit usually should have gone to my private tutors. I could not think of much to credit the public school teachers. Mr. Crowder thought he could eventually convince them that my mind was quite normal, but they were not ready to believe that. My slowness was evidence that I was inferior. *And the file is thick with this truth!* they'd say. In my own opinion, I did feel sorry for myself, and their biased beliefs did work on me, making my school work difficult. Yes, cruel picking at me was certainly a part of it.

My classes at Rye Neck were in English, biology, math, global studies, earth science, and with a little history and civics. I read newspapers and listened to the news each day on television, so I was able to converse quite well on any of those topics. I did have trouble with earth sciences because they wanted us to learn the layers of the earth, and all those terribly long and difficult names of the layers were very hard for me to pronounce or to remember. Dad explained their Latin origin and how they mostly were related to Spanish words, and in that way, I was able to remember them better. When they threatened me with low grades, Dad kept reminding them that school was my whole life. One Miss Lachman was unduly nasty when she telephoned my father. She threatened to fail me, saying "It's time to pay the piper." She was treating me like a ghetto thug, not giving me credit for anything, and she talked to Dad as if he had no brains. Dad took objection to her attitude, and complained officially. Then she counter-complained, saying she had done nothing wrong. But she had! She treated me and Noel (the only other Spanish guy in our class) as if we were unworthy just by being Puerto Rican. Well, they took me out of her class and found me other work to do. Noel as well left her class. (The school was willing to have the two of us suffer a loss in our studies, while never disciplining the teacher, who was the real devil!)

In all of my classes I seldom got credit for true effort, my progress or my steady hard work. Dad considered transferring me to a Catholic school, but at the moment the Catholic high schools in my vicinity were all booked up. He also looked at St. Agnes' School in Manhattan right near the UN. The staff was courteous and eager to have me, but he was fearful for me because he felt the boy students there looked like the typical New York City teenagers, vulnerable to many criminal acts like drugs, knives or crime. He knew I was clean

71

but he also considered me weak in judgment, in that I was a bit longing for friendships, and in that condition of weakness, he felt an unguarded kid could go the wrong way.

One of my problems was over-confidence of my abilities, and good character. I had boasted that I was honest, that I would never rob, but Dad pointed out to me that I had robbed. Once he gave me $80 for a school trip to Washington, and on the day of the trip I had not a penny of it. Yet, I had a new radio and lied and told him I had borrowed it from a friend. He knew I was lying. He'd punish me most for trying to pull the wool over his eyes, and not respecting him as a real parent. Once when he was at the Flushing house, I disappeared. He called and called and nobody answered the phone. So he drove the thirty miles again that day. He was surprised to find nobody home. He waited up for me until midnight, then when I came in, he gave me a sound smack on the face. I had gone out to a party without asking permission or telling him where I was. He said that was very disrespectful.

I threatened twice to run away on him, and once I did. It was the time when my half-brother Charlie was sent to us to keep while the family went to Atlantic City. Mr. Crowder didn't know Charlie, but he was nice to him. After spending the morning playing with my new Nintendo game, that afternoon we were allowed to go to the movies and to have dinner out alone. Charlie was acting suspicious of him, and convinced me that we should run away that night. While Mr. Crowder was upstairs on his floor, watching television, we left his house, leaving the front door wide open. He thought we had gone to the Sugar Pond where kids fish. When I didn't come in at midnight, he got worried. But he didn't call the police. Eventually, he got in touch with my grandmother. No, she didn't know where I was. Mr. Crowder spent a sleepless night. The next day the family found me and Charlie. I had taken us on a train ride and a long expensive taxi-ride to my stepmother's apartment in the Bronx. She got me back to my grandmother and when they called Mr. Crowder, he would not come and get me. He said that since I had gone on my own steam, I had to get back on my own steam. I was going through a crisis about him being my father. When I finally got back to him, I apologized as my grandmother had told me to do. Now he talked sharply , telling me that he was now my family and that I was lucky that he didn't mind my seeing my original family. But, he said, I had to respect him first. He said he would not tolerate my putting my mother, my

72

brothers, my cousins or others in my family before him. He said I had to realize he was spending all his time on me, and I was eating his food and taking his money. I could not defecate on him as I was doing. Yes, I had to learn respect. Well, I knew I had to put him in a higher position in my mind. He loved me and treated me swell. I was a bit of a ghetto thug for not realizing it sooner. I now understood that I did owe him something more in respect.

In Hastings Dad belonged to a parent group for Learning Disabled children. He enjoyed friendship with Mary Curane, Trixie and Dennis, John and Ann, Bernadette, and their meetings, but he didn't see the group making much progress with the tough political structure in the town's educational setup. Those running things in the school system seemed rather wreckless spenders, and basically thirsty title-seekers. He was not at all impressed with the way the top administrators looked at local school needs or the families paying the ridiculously high school taxes. Mostly the teachers and the administrators thought they had a free hand to do as they pleased in school matters, and with the children. They and the School Board couldn't care less about what happened to LD students, and they were very hardheaded about not seeing the need for changes in procedures. Nevertheless, the parent group did some good. Related to my own case, they got the authorities to establish a special ed class at the high school that year. I was asked if I would want to return to Hastings High in September. I thought about it. It would mean I would have three more hours every day, either for sleep, study or just relaxing. It seemed worthwhile, so I said 'yes', I wanted to go back to school in my town. I'd be leaving my good friend, Jason. The Indian girl I was interested in, Shireen, had already transferred. We had quarelled any way. She was pushing me too hard, and Dad had told administrators (defensively) that I was a quiet shy boy not really interested in girls. That was true. They had found my name written on the walls in the girls' toilet, and some thought I had done it!

In spite of my terrible nevi scars running right into my face, some thought I was handsome. When people said that, it made me blush. Dad too thought I was a well-behaved handsome kid; he was proud of me. As he knew I was ashamed of how I look, he had me go into Westchester Community Hospital for my first laser operation on my scars. They decided to start with the ones on my arm and cheek. As I was under Medicaid, being a sort of charity patient, they wanted

73

to experiment on me. That is, the operation would be performed with the senior surgeon right there, but he would be letting his students work on me. One girl, handling a laser gun for the first time, put a serious burn on my arm. It was swollen and blistered, and never went away! When told, the doctor just patted my arm, smilingly, and gave me cortisone salve. The scar is still there and worse than the original scar!

About this time Dad had a visitor from Switzerland. Beautiful and proper Leila Straumann, whose mother, Rubella Manuel, had been a public administration officer in the UN before marrying and moving to Switzerland. Leila's grandfather had been the mayor of Basel. He also owns a Swiss watch factory which is the biggest industry in the small town where they live. While well past eighty, the elder Mr. Straumann, Leila's grandfather, had recently visited China. His house was full of priceless Russian icons. His son Kurt's house was just above, on a hill. I had visited their lovely home in Waldenburg, and met Leila's brother, Alexander. I had also met the head of the Boy Scouts over there, and had my picture taken with him. At the time of Leila's visit, I was so busy at school, I did not see her. Dad took her to a fancy lunch at the Delegates' Dining Room in the UN. She was just in New York two days. When I talk to these upper-class kids (and they are my friends) *none of them* are having trouble in school as I am having. The trouble cannot be me. I think white kids in American schools, from upper-class families, would never have the troubles I have in schools because the system respects upper-class white people.

That April, Dad decided to take me on my second cruise. We'd take the *Queen of Bermuda* again, this time to Key West and Mexico. First, we had an air trip to New Orleans. After touring the city we got on our ship. We had a beautiful large stateroom, up high, on the same deck with the captain, and I enjoyed hearing him speak German to my father. And I was delighted to see familiar faces in the crew! As before, we were invited to the captain's parties and I enjoyed my bit of adulthood, sipping Shirley Temples. Again, it was a lively ship. Meals were great and every night I'd go to the big show in the lounge. Larry Larkin, the comic, this time became my friend. He was from England , had a daughter, and gave me his home address. I was thrilled he kind of joked at me during the shows.

Palm trees and sand greeted us in Key West, and lots of people. Dad and I did some shopping , then he took me to the church, and on to the Hemingway House where he showed me the six-toed kittens (they were freer than we LD kids!). We also saw where the gulf and ocean met, and where President Truman used to stay. I also had my first alcoholic drink, a Pina Colada. Dad went into Sloppy Joe's, got the drinks, then we sat outside on the curb enjoying ourselves alone.

Back on the Gulf once again, most people enjoyed eating or playing bingo. Dad did a lot of reading. I hung out in the pool. I met a couple of nice people my own age, but I was too shy to ask for their home addresses.

Every night I'd go to the disco. One night I stayed out after the disco had closed. At one a.m., Dad, very worried, went around the ship looking for me. He scolded me sharply for this poor judgment, but I was allowed to enjoy the rest of the trip as if nothing had happened. Next we visited Playa del Carmen, a little beachtown in Mexico. Our ship anchored in deep water and a little boat called a 'tender' pulled up aside to get us loaded on. The sea was rough, and the two boats were bobbing around, hitting each other, and one man almost got his arm broken when he jumped from the one ship on to the other. I took my descent bravely, and Dad told me:"You always learn things in traveling. As much as your teachers teach you!" Some of the people from our ship went off to see the Aztec ruins. Dad and I elected to go to CanCun, riding there on a rickety native bus, seeing green bananas on the way. The bus driver sold us American Coca-colas for pesos equivalent to one dollar. In Cancun we visited a big bazaar, then had a delightful time on the beach. Next, we went to the island of Cozumel. More shopping, and I went alone for my first bit of snorkeling. Dad had had sessions with the snorkeling coach and with the ship's nurse to make sure it would be all right for me (with my rather bad asthma problem). In the end, I wasn't afraid. I enjoyed it immensely. Close by was a seventy-year-old California lady also snorkeling for the first time; she was one of our tablemates at dinner.

All around Mexico we of course talked some Spanish, and local people were very friendly to Dad and me. We found them more friendly than white people at home. Much more. On our trip back through New Orleans we stayed two days at the New Orleans Hilton, and got very good service. Much better than the service given nonwhites in New York. Dad took me to Toulouse Street for hush-puppies at Ralph & Kacoo's. I was a bit disturbed by dancing of

Negro boys outside the cathedral. Dancing for pennies. They had been doing this since slavery times. I blamed the white man for not giving them jobs! Dad told me if they didn't soon let me get proficient in a skill or academic subject, it could happen to me. **A loser with nothing.** On the whole, up North, maybe we did have it better in schooling. At least in some places where racism wasn't so strong among teachers. Yes, my own situation was grave. By consistently misjudging my work, teachers could leave me with no credentials and no complete education, no more than these boys had.

Dad kind of foresaw that I would continue to have trouble in school, so one night he told me quietly that we would do a lot of traveling. It was his plan to take me everywhere he had been, and he had been all over the world. I knew that all this was difficult for him because, soon after I came, he began getting very ill. He had been taking high blood pressure medication for 15 years and had discovered on his own that it was killing him. Doctors had tried a dozen different drugs but none of them worked; they all made his pressure go higher. So, on his own he learned that with proper eating and vitamins, one could keep a lower blood pressure and good health. But by this time, from the drugs, his kidneys and liver had been ruined. When I heard him coughing in the night, I became concerned, but he was in good spirits and a good doctor for himself. I knew he was mainly concerned for me. He wanted me to keep in good health, and be prepared when his old age came; and, he wanted me to grow up with an education. I did my best to get ready, and to please him.

***** ***** *****

At Disneyland, California.
(r.top) With Wangs of Red
China.
(r.mid)With Dr. Howard and
the Aokis in SanFrancisco.
Our house being enlarged for
Me (Nov.1987).

CHAPTER SEVEN

True enough, that summer of 1989, we were set for a whirlwind of traveling. First we went to Europe, arriving in Brussels, Belgium on 21st of June. We took time to see the Grand Platz and the Cathedral. The big old church was under renovation. The door was open, others were going in, so we went in. But the foreman on the job came quickly, yelling and cursing, and he made us leave. We then realized there were racial feelings in Brussels. You could see sitting around the city a lot of black Africans, looking poor and out of work. So, America was not the only one with racial problems. Then when my father went to check our bags so that we would not have to carry them around town, instead of counting the cost in coins, he merely held out a large hand of coins and the white attendant took every penny, and we both knew this too was racism as the coins Dad had were about ten times the cost of leaving luggage. Next, we had spaghetti dinner at an Arab place and they treated us very nice. When we went to a museum, caretakers began watching us closely, as if we had come there to steal. This was my experience in Belgium.

We went on train to Germany and Dad had no trouble with the two languages spoken by the conductors. We had comfortable quarters and when the train was due, it arrived precisely on the minute at the large station in Cologne. We called our friend, Peter Jakob, who lived a few miles away in Neuss. While he was coming for us we went to the American MacDonald's that was just across the street from the Köln Dom (cathedral). We were delighted having a hamburger, and a strawberry shake that was better than any strawberry shake we had had in America. Peter and his two kids, Judie and Matthias, came to greet us. Right away Dad started talking German, and I had to listen and try to understand it. In spite of my American teachers marking me down, I do __very well__ with languages. Within three days I was speaking German with the Jakob kids.

We went everywhere in Germany and there is no time here to give details of our sightseeing other than to say the Jakobs were very gracious hosts. They gave us the third floor of their house which had been her father's apartment when he came down from Berlin after her mother died. I learned that in previous visits Dad and Mr. Berg had had many long conversations , in German, about Hitler times, talking together like old friends. Evelin's father had been a painter, and on our last day she parted with one of his alpine paintings as a gift to Dad.

I must tell you, in these days i was a Boy Scout addict; I didn't go anywhere without wearing my Scouts' uniform. Well, one day when Dad and I had been alone in Düsseldorf, (he wanted to show me König's Allee and the old Krupp building). While we were going back to Neuss, I caused a lot of commotion. One German pushed me because of the uniform. Another young German came over to talk to me. He had been a Boy Scout once, but he said people in Germany did not like uniforms now. Well, the Jakobs never told me that. Nevertheless, I did not take off my uniform. I'd rather have them look at me for it , than staring for my race, or my scars, as was the case in Belgium.

One of my Dad's friend, Monica, had been a chorister in a German choir which had sung in the United States. Monica and her new husband, gave a garden party for us at her new home. It was a barbecue, and she was growing many nice things in her garden. Dad drank rosé wine, then champagne. I was a little worried about his kidneys, but he was all right. Next day Dad and I went walking in the village, to buy fruit and flowers. One grocery lady gave him a hard time because of his dark face, but when he spoke sharply to her in German, she behaved. That afternoon Judie took me bicycling: she and I alone; we were out more than an hour, managing nicely in our cross-English-German language. (*Listen all you racist teachers in New York! See what I can do? And you'd give me* **no credit** *for anything -always bad marks!*)

Next, Dad and I got on train and rode down to Switzerland, to see our good friends, the Straumanns. Rubella met us at the Basel train station, and right away a three-day twirl of sightseeing began. They wanted to take us to ski country, but the snow was light this year. We went to Interlaken and Lucerne instead. We had to get back to Germany that weekend as Dad had an important meeting in Bonn, to see a member of government, Mr. von Welck, who had been an interne under Dad at the UN. We had a delightful time with Hubertus and Sybil. They had been in Zimbabwe and their house in

Konigswinter was filled with many African souvenirs. I was impressed upon learning that her family owned one of those lovely castles we had seen when going down the Rhine on our way to Switzerland. Oh, by the way, in Basel train station I met a number of Boy Scouts on their way to a jamboree in Denmark. The guys from Mexico enjoyed talking Spanish with me.

Back in New York, Dad had a Jewish wedding to do. I became moody, worrying about the approaching school year. He encouraged me to go swimming at the Hastings pool. We also visited the Natural History Museum and a Greek place on Broadway that made fantastic spaghetti. Dad gave me no time to feel depressed. Soon, in August, we were off flying again, this time to Michigan. Ours was a fancy hotel down east on the Detroit River; we could get around from there. Dad showed me the house on LeMay Street where his good friend, Terry Little, the Las Vegas Hilton entertainment boss, grew up. On our visit to St. Paul's Cathedral, Dad saw a beautiful elderly lady he knew, Mrs. Webster, who had been his mother's good friend and classmate at Spelman College. I felt good meeting yet another generation of his family's friends, someone who knew his mother, because, from all I heard, she was a great lady.

Being in Detroit with all his old friends was very relaxing. And it makes me feel important. Mr. Proctor's sister, Eloise, invited us to dinner; she lived out in the old West Side where Dad grew up. Now it was all Afro-American but very neat houses, with grass and flowers. And I saw Sampson, the second grade school he attended. Miss Proctor , at age near ninety, had been one of the first colored school teachers in Detroit. This day she cooked a fantastic ham and chicken meal, and had about ten people to dinner. At her advanced age, this was great! She asked me about school; I didn't want to talk. People assume northern schools are all okay, especially those who knew the South and how whites treat dark people down there. While Detroit had its whites running away from blacks, what we faced in New York, this constant hatred pushing, and nasty teachers always marking us down, ours was disgraceful behavior even Detroiters couldn't understand. What could I say, really? I said nothing.

The highlight of our trip this time was a fancy wedding reception we went to with the Proctors. Dad knew the bride's mother, Honey. The bride was very beautiful. I thought she looked Spanish.

She had just married a young man from Spain. This was a society wedding. The girl's father was a millionaire. When we got back home in New York, Dad sent her a crystal candleholder from Sweden, and another piece of crystal for the Proctors.

Well, after all this world traveling, my mood began to improve. I actually felt elated in September to be back at my old school, a part of which was Hastings High School. The new so-called special education class was a strange mixture. Our teacher, Miss Ross, was very nice, but the kids seemed to be a glum-looking hodge-podge of people, different ages, different backgrounds and different readiness. Mostly it was a black class, majority coming from the foster care homes at the edge of town, and not an example at all of the upper-class families of Hastings who paid the taxes. When I explained it to Dad, he told me to be careful about what I said in class, that these kids were not like the kids I went to school with in Rye Neck. They'd resent the good things of our life. But be friendly, if possible!

Well, his true words only had a few days to sink in before two black boys (and a Spanish boy) from one of the homes decided to pick on me. They'd laugh and make fun of me. I thought I was strong but when you get this pestering every day, it becomes hard to take. My teachers knew it was going on, but they did nothing. When finally my father came in to talk to Mr. Sobet, the psychologist, he was told that James had to fend for himself, that it was natural for kids in school to pick on others. This of course was not true. The normal kids in the normal classes did not have this, and they did not have my scars. As my father said, why live in a good neighborhood to have a child suffer ghetto-like circumstances in his class! The atmosphere was all wrong for me. The planners for Hastings High's ungraded special ed class had never thought of this being a **downward** step for some of us. In other words, it began to look like I'd be getting an inferior education in this setup. Dad says part of one's inspiration comes from one's exposure to others and the interchange of conversation and knowledge. With my lifestyle being unknown to these kids, it seems we had no common ground. Miss Ross, the teacher, seemed to realize this and she gave me more personal time. Nevertheless, I was suffering in this situation and Dad noticed it in my loss of enthusiasm. One day I came home crying and said I wanted to transfer back to Rye Neck. He understood, and he told me he'd talk to school authorities as soon as he returned from a short trip to Detroit, to see his dentist.

Dad told school authorities about his three-day trip and the fact that he had arranged for my care. And what he told me was that if the black boys kept bothering me, I had his permission to stay home and he would straighten it out once he returned. He was staying at the Hilton in Windsor, Ontario, and we'd talk daily on the phone. I never told him anything but when he got back he learned from two neighbors that there had been trouble at the school. Yes, the black boys had bothered me and I stayed home *one day* and just as soon as I did, the school sent the police for me! They went all over town looking for me. When Dad heard this he hit the ceiling. He told them to call a school meeting, and they did, with the Guidance people attending and the assistant principal. Right away they were ready to put Dad in his place. The guidance woman told him that he was not to leave children unattended , and that he could go to jail for it. Dad said he did not need to explain details of what he had privately arranged for my care and that their talk was mere supposition. He further told them that it was not right the way they let the personal attacks continue on me, doing nothing. He also took Miss Heinrick to task for calling the cops on me. My absence from school was my first and only time. I was not truant. I was ill at ease, taking a day off, sitting in the park. If she was to call anybody, why didn't she call a priest? He ended his remarks saying they'd never do that to a Jewish student in town. They got the message, and all of them became real nasty to me. So, that January, I transferred back to Rye Neck High School.

My friend, Jason, was glad to see me, and, somewhat Miss Trasda as well. I quickly adapted to the old routine, up at 6:30, wait for the bus, Valhalla in the morning, Rye Neck in afternoons, home at 4, then study with my tutors. . .all this, until bedtime. And soon, as before, the delinquency reports began coming to my father. But, in spite of them, he liked the Rye Neck bunch better than the Hastings bunch who had given me a steady stream of demerits. Mostly from the administrators, not the teachers. Once Miss Ross let us out early and told us we could go home, because there was a football pep rally. The administrative man who bothered me about the bathroom, saw me going home, grabbed me and brought me back to school, and I got a demerit even though I attended the football rally as he demanded. He wouldn't listen to me when I told him the teacher had dismissed us and told us we could go home. A minority kid is always punished unduly like that.

Now I was missing my good Hastings teachers. In middle school it had been Miss Tibbs. In high school it had been Miss Harman , the cooking teacher, and Miss Newman, the arts teacher. I also liked Mrs. Krim, my speech lady, but she did me dirty by turning me in for a demerit. Dad hated to see me leave Miss Ross, because, like Miss Tibbs, she gave me good grades, and helped me. Also at Hastings I had a chance to show my real ability. As a member of the Key Club, I was elected to be host when a group of Russian athletes visited our school. I had to make a speech to welcome them. That morning, I asked Dad to write down a few Russian words of greeting for me. I tried saying them, and he corrected me. At school, I was bold enough to try those words, and the Russians liked it! *They understood my speaking their language!* But no teacher gave me praise (*another record says **I cannot talk**, not even in English!*).

I got used to the stricter setup at Rye Neck, but I noticed there was more criticism of me than the others. By now, Dad was in direct touch with BOCES headquarters, and he was sorry to learn Miss Wilma Gilbert had retired. She was a fair person, a good supervisor. Now back in the Rye Neck prestige mill of Who-Is-Qualified-to-Succeed, I had no backup good person. Dad knew the school would keep him busy that year with pettiness and threats.

In the autumn of 1989 we got a new Oldsmobile and it made me feel great whenever we drove around the kids hanging out at the high school in Hastings. And for Christmas Dad had given me a guitar and I right away started private lessons in Dobbs Ferry. So I moved into 1990 feeling more mature in my learning. And, I wasn't as sick as I had been before. The morning sneezing had just about disappeared. At the end of February we went to Florida, for a breath of spring. It was fun but I was anxious to get back to my guitar. It had become a daily bit of relaxing for me. I enjoyed imitating the Rock guys I saw on television. Once, I banged that thing terribly hard, breaking most of the strings. (I called it being *hyper*.) Dad was sore at me because he had watched me destroy a watch that way, and a compass. I also was rather belligerent when doing the dishes, and I broke several of Dad's antique things.

Without a doubt, music was something special for me. My guitar teacher, Tom Giglio, was great, and he never complained like the public school teachers complain. I was learning a lot about music, as Dad was teaching me piano, and made me practice from time to time. Three days a week now I would be home alone, because Dad had to get to the Flushing house for work he had to do there. I was learning to care for myself. Only when there was a heavy rain, I sometimes got frightened. And I kept a big baseball bat by my bed, in case some intruder came. In spite of school authorities' criticisms, what Dad was trying to do for me was to make me self-reliant. And I didn't object at all to being alone. However, once I overslept, and the bus driver kept blowing his horn. Neighbors complained to Dad.

Soon I had my second laser operation. This one would be on my forehead; half of its skin was to come off. Dad insisted that the major surgeon work on me, no trainees! I was worried too because those hot laser guns would be right up next to my eyes (and I only had one eye). Well, we prayed and everything went all right. Back in school once the bandages were off, kids were complimenting me on the improvement in my looks.

Soon Miss Trasda sent home a letter to Dad saying I was failing. She didn't even put his name on it, but rather said:"To the Guardian of James. . ." He called her and let her know that he was no longer the 'guardian', that James was his rightful son. On the issue of failure, she was playing her usual game: threats, threats, threats. My favorite teacher, as I've told you, was Mr. Hubschman, my gym teacher. He was always great to me. Always gave me 100% as a grade. He kidded me and had me helping him do things. Once with another student I had to move a heavy garbage bin, and I came down ill with muscle spasms. Dad wrote him a note and he never complained like other teachers, and he never punished me with a low grade.

In early April I got very ill. Some kind of choking cough. Dad had told the doctor that my asthma attacks improved when I took antibiotics and finally the doctor let us have some tetracycline on hand. So, this time when Dad gave me the medicine, I did not improve. He had been ill with a similar cough, but he had gotten over it. Mine lingered on and on, and the worse thing about this, we were scheduled to go to London on vacation in a matter of days. One night the attack was so bad that Dad rushed me at midnight to Dobbs Ferry Hospital. The Chinese doctor there gave me an antibiotic and let me go home. He had taken chest pictures and Dad had asked him if it were all right for me to travel soon. I had no fever so the doctor said okay. However, when we got to London, I was sicker than before. Dad consulted the hotel manager and he recommended a local doctor. We took a taxi to his office. Dr. Gormley had some fifteen patients waiting, but he took me first! And he charged us not a dime! His prescription for me was Augmentin. He said it had more bite as a mixture of several drugs, and I needed this to kill my bronchial pneumonia germs. It worked! And with British tea which we had practically every hour, I felt better in a matter of hours. But we were slow on sightseeing. I only saw Windsor Castle, Hampton Court, a few discos in Leicester Square, Tower Hill, London Bridge and Big Ben. It was Easter time and we did not get to St. Paul's as Dad wished. We went instead to Catholic St. Michael's. We did get to see Harrod's, and down in the same area, Baden Powell's house. I met a Boy Scout from Switzerland and an elderly man Boy Scout (former priest) from Germany. We had lunch there, and viewed the glass cases containing the history of scouting. One evening we had tickets to "Les Miserables", but unfortunately, I was sick again, and we had to walk out in the middle of this expensive and enjoyable show.

In spite of my illness, I liked London. The people seemed so much more civilized than New Yorkers (or New York teachers!). Finally relieved about the upturn in my health, Dad made me get a good rest once we were home again. As usual, I went with him on his many guest appearances as organist in Westchester churches. That summer, I started going out with a new girl, Lisa, whom I had met at BOCES. She lived some eighteen miles away. Dad would take me there, then, he'd have to come back for me at the end of the day. Once when he came back to pick me up at six, I wasn't there. He drove back home. At 8:45 I called him saying "You can come and get me now." He really scolded me this time. I had him driving almost a hundred miles that day, without ever realizing it. He told me I was too selfish. And, he didn't like it that I would let a girl monopolize my weekends so completely. He told me that later when I have a job, my own money and my own car, I could go out with someone living at distance, but right now, it was too much for him. Lisa was blond and pretty, but it was never a racial matter.

In late May, Dr. Wang, now working in Canada, came down from Toronto to spend a few days with us. He was going steady and came to see his girlfriend, Christine, someone from Vietnam. As usual, we went out to have some good Chinese food. For my birthday on July 7th Dad took me to Oscar's in the Waldorf-Astoria hotel. We went there often, and the nice Spanish waitress knew us. It was a beautiful day, and we also celebrated Dad's birthday which fell on the 8th. Two days later, he was very sick, with one of his kidney problems, and blood pressure. But he had a good way of taking care of himself. Usually a long sitz bath would bring him around.

That August, Dad and I visited Weilin in Canada. We decided to go by Amtrak. It was a hot day when we left, and unusual for Dad, he'd go in shirtsleeves, i.e. without his suit jacket. Each of us had a medium-big suitcase. Well, when we changed subway trains in Jackson Heights, somebody pushed behind Dad and he knew immediately that his wallet had been stolen. Three young white fellows were standing near us, but he could not accuse them. Immediately when we got out at Grand Central Station he went to the telephones and tried to call Chemical Bank to stop any usage of our credit card. Actually, the wallet contained credit cards, driver's license, university papers and some money but not all. He had trip money in a suitcase and that was our saving grace, as we could continue our trip. A guard in Chemical Bank at Grand Central promised to help us by notifying the credit card people, since we could not get through and it was train time. With such a great loss, Dad still remained cheerful. He said it was only the second time in his life that he had been so "wiped out".

The train was crowded with West Indians going up for an ethnic celebration in Toronto. The authorities at the border held the train for two hours, checking all these West Indians' papers. It was said too many of them were making the trip planning to stay, and the Canadian Government didn't want this. Our poor friend was at Union Station waiting for us in spite of our being long overdue. After going to nice meals and several Toronto museums we drove down to Niagara Falls. It was my first trip, and I was allowed to enter the United States from the Canadian side. When we said good-bye to Dr. Wang several days later, we got back on the train and rode through Detroit, not getting off. Actually it was some little town north of Detroit. With all that beautiful Michigan Central Station in Detroit, closed up now (because of racism), the trains went around Detroit, mostly. We were on our way to Chicago to visit John Gehm, my father's good friend from his Columbia University days. Mr. Gehm and his Swedish wife, Gail, lived in Northbrook, a suburb of Chicago.

They were very friendly and relaxed; it was as if I had known them all my life. They gave me a big surprise: I was allowed to have sleeping in my room their huge Alaskan dog I call Kojak. He was tan and white, very friendly, and made me realize I had always loved animals. Second day we went down to Michigan Avenue and all the museums. The streets were clean; the Union Station was clean (Dad took me there, remembering long layovers there with his mother, going South in the 1930s). We had lunch with Dr. Heather Chen, from China, who used to live at Dad's house in Flushing. She was glad to see us, and told us her big secret: she was soon to get married to a Dr. Ruben, an American, and move to Washington, D.C.

I met Mr. Gehm's three kids, Eric with his fancy sportscar, Michel, the beauty, and Lisa, the doctor. Here again were friends Dad had known for over thirty years. Next, we were off for Detroit. As Amtrak sped across lower Michigan, I was able to see the big Kellogg setup in Battle Creek. While train-riding I relaxed, listening to my tapes, especially Guns 'n Roses new "November Rain". I also read my crazy stuff, this time "Satan Wants You". I laughed out, remembering how one day I got bored on the long busride home from school, and I started talking witch-talk to the kids. The driver excitedly called my father and had him meet the bus. Dad lectured me: satan talk was not acceptable. Period.

Dad also read on train, as we crossed Michigan at a fast rate. Soon we reached Detroit and we backed into this miserable little wooden shack they were using as a train station, while the big beautiful stone and marble real station (closed) was just a stone's throw away. Detroiters were used to all these condemnations when whites moved to the suburbs. That big beautiful Hudson's department store, downtown, closed. This time we'd be staying downtown in the fancy guest apartment of the Proctors, down on the river, with a splendid view of Canada. We had the place all to ourselves as they were in their family home north of the city. I was happy to see our cousin Lawrence again, and Dr. Fuller. On our train ride into New York, early-morning fog hung low on the marshes. And the Hudson was beautiful. Soon we passed right through Hastings, our home, and the white lady we were talking to didn't believe us. She said:"Oh-h, that's too rich for you!"

*****   *****   *****

CHAPTER EIGHT

I have already told you I was careless about picking up, as many teenagers are. Also, I would tear down mechanical things (like bicycles) and never put them back together. This irritated Dad because he was nothing like this. But we, more or less, had the same disposition, the same calm. Another thing, he was good in handling money. I was a bit careless with money. Once at Hastings High , I put twenty dollars in my pocket, and lost it. Also I had an uncanny habit of spending recklessly on tapes. Then when he got me a compact disc outfit, I began spending heavily on discs. I wasn't saving anything of my allowance. And Dad had told me: never, never spend your last dollar, and I often did. He'd punish me a bit, and would check my secret place to see whether my saved money was still there. I knew he had financial problems of his own. At the rental house in Flushing tenants assumed he had money and would steal from us. Usually he had two students at a time, but occasionally it got up to three , and when someone would leave in mid-semester, often there'd only be one person in the house. And, once or twice, nobody was there and we'd have the place all to ourselves. Dad learned a lot about human nature in renting rooms to students. One guy moved in and paid one week's rent, and stayed three months and never paid again. Dad first wrote him several notes, then packed up all his stuff from his room. (We found bullets and notices from the police.) In the end, we had to change the locks because Mike kept our keys and kept coming back. Another student (from China) was very rude. He'd go into Dad's room searching and stealing things ,and he'd disobey the rules by cooking at midnight. Nevertheless, Dad preferred Chinese students. He said that on the whole, they were the best. More respect for you!

Dad disliked having Americans most; both blacks and whites could be bad medicine. Arabs would take over and try to get their friends in. We had Indians who wouldn't follow the rules, and leave things messy. We had Orientals who'd overstock the kitchen. Dad liked most South Americans but some were 'cheap', thinking we had too much money. But you could not generalize when it came to world

88

people; some would stop up the toilets and break things, others would be friendly and a pleasure to have; or, two types : (a) careful, respectful people, (b) careless disrespectful people. The most agonizing problem was the telephone. We kept them open and people were calling all over the world, not telling Dad, and he'd have to draw money out of his savings to pay the phone bills. As bills came in a month later, very often the persons making all those calls had moved. So, Dad lectured me on how to keep a good house , concerned now about my future. I knew he planned to leave this house to me, but he wanted me in a profession. And the schools were not getting me ready , not ready for anything concrete.

That September, we took Mrs. Cheatham, my guardian, to a fancy dance party at United Nations. A few days later, we had a visitor from Sweden, Mrs. Asbrink. She was originally from Brazil but married a Swedish man. She owned a boutique over there and was in New York shopping for new things. She carried her money in a belt around her stomach. One day Dad let me take her to the shops in our small town. Well, when she got back, she suddenly felt her waist and yelled: "My money!" The purse was empty. We went rushing back to the stores, then later she realized she had put her money elsewhere. Happy for her, that evening Dad called Sue Walsh and we had a dinner party at the Chart House on the river in Dobbs Ferry. Dad was impressed when a nice girl waiting tables there spoke to me. He was always afraid that I did not have too many friends. Kevin now (from Boy Scouts) was playing football, and we didn't socialize.

Dad had two cat scans and learned he had a benign growth on his liver. Now he'd read more on health. I kept a watchful ear whenever I heard him coughing in the night. Soon he went back to Detroit for a dental appointment. He stayed at the Hilton near the airport and would call me every one of the three days. Now I could function very well by myself. Whereas he once worried that I might have a major attack, I now knew that if I did, the main thing was to keep calm and breathe carefully. He made me keep all my necessary medicines near my bed. Upon occasions he was playing for Lois Morton, the organist at the fancy Bronxville Church of Christian Science. I'd always go with him. And, yes, we were taking in some of Mary Baker Eddy's message.

We both had memberships in the White Plains YMCA. He went during the week and I came with him on Sundays. While he was in the weight-lifting room I'd be alone in the gym or at the handball courts. One white man pushed me; another took my ball away from me. Dad and I both knew that racism was growing in the New York area. At school I was still getting a barrage of criticism. Other than Mr. Hubschman, I liked Mr. McKenzie. But occasionally he'd go along with the criticisms of me. Once I lashed back at him and Dad made me apologize.

For Christmas that year, 1990, we went to Puerto Rico. Before getting me, Dad used to go every winter, but he hadn't been in ten years and it surprised him to find everything still nice, clean and aromatic, as it used to be. We stayed at Olimpo Court hotel in San Turce where he had stayed many times. We had our own kitchen and could eat in. He sent me out grocery-shopping alone. With my iffy Spanish, I was able to do all right! I was happy to be in the land of my ancestors. I loved Old San Juan. The fortress, El Morro, had been built by blacks! I also liked El Yunque, the rain forest. Dad allowed me to get another watch from a Chinese jewelry shop. Careless at school, I had lost two calculators, a gold chain, and a watch. On Christmas Eve the Puerto Ricans were down below my window making beautiful guitar music at midnight. On Christmas Day we went to a small church nearby. No one was there and we had the ancient splendor all to ourselves. I wished my grandmother or mother could have been with us.
　　Once when I was walking with Dad on the beach near Ashford Avenue someone yelled: "James! James!!" It was Andy from my Boy Scouts troop! He was down there on a swimming meet. We were glad to see each other. Dad told me the same thing had happened to him in Kyoto, Japan - somebody called him as he got off the bullet train in that crowded railroad station. On our Mexican cruise, a lady at our table, Lois, knew Howard Darling, the organist from White Plains. The world is small! Deja vu. Yes, I remember some French, though my teachers say I know nothing about languages! Or, about the world!

As 1991 started I followed the Persian Gulf War. Dad got me a couple Desert Storm t-shirts, and I wore them proudly. Crown Heights disturbed me quite a bit because the Jews and Blacks should not be fighting. That spring, Dad enrolled in a computer course at Queensboro College. He had no trouble; he said the course was interesting. Little did I know then that I soon would be in that school, having all sorts of troubles!

On Monday, April 22, 1991 something terrible happened at school. I was hit by a hockey stick in gym. It put a big gash in my head, and the ambulance came and took me to United Hospital in Portchester. They called Dad and he rushed over. The doctor who sewed me up was good, so there was no worry there, but Dad was worried that maybe some damage had occurred to my brain or eyes. The school became very nasty, sending him the medical bills, but he flatly refused to pay, knowing they had insurance coverage. Also that April, one of our Detroit friends, golden teacher Eloise Proctor, died. We were saddened even though she was near ninety. And just a few months earlier she had been so alive! I worried now about myself. Dad soon would be dead, and I would have no one, and the schools were not letting me get educated properly. God, please help me! I want to take care of myself, and be useful in the world.

That spring Dad was playing often for Kathryn Jones and Rev. Shepherd at Ardsley Methodist. He also was guest organist at three prestigious society churches in Westchester: the Congregational Church in Briarcliff Manor, Scarsdale Baptist and St. James the Less. In Scarsdale, the music went beautifully and ladies applauded him. He felt a highpoint in his music sub-career, telling me that it was something in his youth he'd always wanted first in his life. But his parents wanted him to be a doctor. And in the end he was neither their first choice nor his first choice. I knew his great organ year was 1984 (before I came to him), when he played concerts in Germany, and aboard the QEII. I felt happy for him. As for myself, I wanted to be anything respectable. I didn't feel I would ever succeed academically because teachers had been too positive making my record so that I could not advance. Even if I couldn't live up to their high expectations, I wouldn't be a nothing. If no good job, I could probably sell off Dad's assets and go back living in the Bronx, back to my poor Spanish neighborhood. I don't think that would be so bad. Our people act nicer, making me feel that somebody loves me.

Dad made plans to send me away for the summer of 1991. I'd be going to our good friend, Judy, who once lived in California. Now she had set herself and her business up in Flagstaff, Arizona, keeping alive her father's name and his music. The trip would be complicated for a normal boy, and especially complicated for someone called Learning Disabled. I'd be going alone. Taking an airplane in New York, getting off at Chicago, changing planes at O'Hare Airport, flying to Phoenix, changing planes again, for Flagstaff. Well, on the incoming trip Judy agreed to meet me by car in Phoenix, but coming home I had to do it all by myself. I was away two weeks, and I had to manage my money, to buy my meals and take care of my needs. In the end I was triumphant. I made it!! All alone!! Mr. Gehm, my Dad's old friend from college, met me at the airport in Chicago, and chatted with me during my stopover. He too was proud of me. But when I told the story at school, I got no compliments.

That September I started my senior year at Rye Neck High School. Dad was saddened when I selected my yearbook picture without even showing him the proofs. Many familylike things I didn't know how to do. And he was equally startled when Lisa's mother called up on Prom night asking where I was. I had never told him I agreed to take her on this dress-up date. Now he lectured me, saying for a girl the Prom was almost as important as her wedding. He made me sit down and write a letter of apology to Lisa and her mother.

More trouble came at school when the psychologist started laughing at me. He was talking about me in front of other people. One day I came home crying and Dad asked me what was the matter. Mr. Lois had discussed me in the classroom right in front of other kids, saying he didn't think I should graduate, and he asked me:"Do you think you're going to graduate? I've got news for you; I'm recommending that you stay on another year." My dad was flabbergasted to hear this, and he made a number of phone calls. When he got to the bottom of it, it seems my friend was partly in the picture. His parents had decided maybe he should stay on for another year, and since I was his friend, the teachers decided maybe I too should stay on another year; they came to this decision making NO DISCUSSION WITH MY FATHER. He, a nonwhite, had to take their decisions. No! Now he was very firm in telling them that he wanted me to graduate on time.

If I had been white, like my friend, this kind of snubbing of the parent would not have happened. Dad reinforced his edict by getting me again a full corps of private tutors. He wanted to make sure I passed all the Regents' exams. Well, the first time, I didn't pass, but I kept working at my reviews. Dad drilled me every night on one subject or another. I was doing quite well remembering science, math and historical facts.

In November Dad had to go to Michigan for the 50th anniversary of his class, and decided to take me along. He had already been in discussion with the university about my chances of getting accepted in the literary college. Well, they invited me for an interview! I was so elated that I told it at school. We formally requested that I be allowed to miss one day of classes to go to Michigan. And as an extra treat, Dad took me to the Michigan-Ohio State football game at the famous Michigan Stadium. 110,000 people. Wow! It was so cold, we left after the half, and had a peaceful bit of relaxing in the Michigan Union clubhouse, with Dad and I playing a game of billiards. That evening we were festive at the German Department's reunion dinner, where I heard some German songs and poetry. That night and the following morning we enjoyed the whirlpool bath at the Radisson in Ypsilanti where we stayed.

The lady who interviewed me at Michigan, Miss Gilmore, said that if I passed all seven of my Regents' tests, I could likely count on being admitted as a freshman at Michigan. This was wonderful news. Dad had already shown me the places where he had lived as a seventeen-year-old student. And we had also put some money down on a co-op apartment in Detroit. But the likelihood was really negative; he would hate to lose me and would want me to go to a college nearer home. Once back in New York my whirlwind review work began again. Schoolbooks every day of the week. To make me appreciate the reward factor, Dad told me, if I passed, he'd take me on a tour of six Caribbean countries. Well, I did put myself fully into my studies while my main teacher kept saying I'd never make it. And Mr. Lois when he saw me one day in the hall, laughingly said:"I hear your father will send you to Harvard!" I at the time did not know what Harvard was. When I told Dad this bit of news, he told me it was a sick joke.

In January 1992, I surprised myself in being the only child in my class to pass all seven Regents' exams. Hurray-y!! I didn't get much praise at the school, but friends and my father were most elated. **I had proved that I was somebody.** And biased teachers could not take this away from me. At the time Dad was getting ready his annual lecture for the Brooklyn chapter of Delta Sigma Theta Sorority. It was their ninth Afro-American Book Fair year, and he enjoyed working with Rose Eiland, Juanita Bobbit, Barbara Haynes and Sylvia Matthew. So on 9th February we battled the raw cold , getting ourselves to the Hanson Place Central Methodist Church. This charitable event was always well-attended, and it greatly helped black authors to become known. Dad allowed me to be a useful person there, managing my own booth. At the semester break, true to his word, Dad took me on a cruise to the Caribbean.

We flew first to Puerto Rico, and I was delighted to be back in the peaceful home of my ancestors. We boarded the Regency Sun there, and sailed to St. Lucia, Martinique, Domenica, St. Kitts, then St. Thomas, Virgin Islands. In St. Lucia I marveled over the strange volcanic mountain peaks rising like black ice cream cones. In Martinique we went up the rugged road of Mt. Pele to see the ancient volcanic ruins of a colorful old town, and our guide told us there were snakes. If bitten, she said, we'd be dead in 24 hours. In St. Kitts, Dad knew the Coury family who owned all the supermarkets, and we visited Louise at the Hardware store they owned. She was very pleased to see us. We sat nearby at a hotel wedding ceremony and visited the Batik factory. I was impressed upon hearing local people talking about two famous people-of-color, Alexander Hamilton , from nearby Nevis, and Josephine, Napoleon's Empress of France, from Martinique. I couldn't talk about this at school; I did wonder why Americans are so set in trying to make history `white'.

Next in St. Thomas we went to visit Alexander Farrelly, the Governor, who had been my father's friend at United Nations. As he was out, we left a note for him with his tough Indian guards. I bought a colorful tiger tapestry for my room. Dad wanted me to street-dance with some P.R. kids, but I was too shy. Back in San Juan we bought two more Haitian paintings and visited the Bombanero which was my favorite old restaurant. We had had a grand vacation, and I thanked Dad profusely. And he was happy for me, knowing now I had a good chance of making it in college.

You have to understand that all this time I was under two school districts, the initial school in Hastings made recommendations about me, and also some matters were decided by Rye Neck where I was in attendance. I got a nice letter from the former, about my passing the Regents' tests, and it said that I had earned the right to have a regular diploma and not an IEP diploma (they usually give LD kids).Yet, evil forces were at work at Rye Neck! They told me I couldn't have a regular diploma, that I had to take and pass a test in occupational skills, and this involved the third school, the people at Valhalla! So, one week before graduation what kind of diploma I'd get was still in question, a mystery. In the last minute, they scheduled the occupational skills test for me, saying I needed to pass it to graduate. The teacher did not have a model test paper I could study at home. She told me to go to my friend Jason's house and study with him. My father saw the hocus-pocus of it and got right on the telephone, calling people. Then Hastings stepped into the picture saying I didn't need the occupational skills test, that I had met other criteria. Well, as the test was already scheduled, I took it. I thought I did okay but Jason told me he knew the results, and I didn't pass.

With the hocus-pocus quickly developing Dad saw that he had to stay firmly in the picture, or else I wouldn't graduate. Yes, he was able to confirm that no matter what, I could graduate without the occupational skills business. And, as he began tackling this business of whether I would get the regular or IEP diploma, he found an unbelievable layer of administrative people involved. First of all, the principals of the schools don't want to be involved. Mine at Rye Neck said she had no jurisdiction, that BOCES was merely 'renting space' there. And BOCES had an unbelievable network of offices and hierarchies. Dad found it easier to go right to Albany. The officials there were more responsive, knowing that Dad meant business. In the end, they threw it back to local people in the Westchester area, but in it we had a new nice lady to deal with, and she (Ms. McMann or McDonald) told my father (in the last 30 hours before graduation) that they were having a big meeting, and she'd call us as soon as it was over. Well, they agreed I'd get my regular diploma! All this fuss about one student, just because his father complained. On that night we had to drive to a new BOCES compound of buildings just north of White Plains, to attend an awards ceremony, (I was receiving the Bob Newman award for an essay I wrote). My teachers attending were stern with me in view of my father's presence. He was the culprit! In the end, thanks to him, I got my regular diploma!

My big day was June 25,1992. Dad had planned to get me a stretch limousine to attend graduation and the after-party he was giving for me at the Waldorf-Astoria in New York. But with all the fuss, he cancelled the limousine, not wanting to draw any attention to me. We came in two family cars, the Oldsmobile and my cousin Tom's white Cadillac. Dad got Mom out of the hospital and brought her, and my dear grandmother also came. We were a handsome

95

family group, including Mr. Crowder, my new dad. People stared at us mainly because my grandmother was as white (and as beautiful) as any of them. So, in my black cap and gown I was happy, yet, I felt like crying too. It had all been such a hard struggle, and Dad and I were fighting right up till the last minute. My main teacher, who had made so much trouble for me, she didn't even bother to come to our graduation ceremony. In fact, I saw none of my teachers there. Other teachers, yes, but none of the teachers who had made me work so hard. None to congratulate me and my Spanish friend, Noel. Jason too got a regular diploma, but still, I was the only one in the BOCES group who had passed all the Regents' tests, and Dad told me never to forget it. He was very proud of me.

***** ***** *****

High School Graduation, June 1992

In Niagara Falls, Canada, 1990

Dad and I on Cruise to Mexico

Me in Orlando, Florida

CHAPTER NINE

As a present for calmly withstanding all the heat, and finally graduating from high school, Dad decided to take me on a world trip, actually a tour of the Far East, as I had been in Europe and Latin America already. He was doing this expressly for me, as he had already been six times around the world. Having reached age seventy, he was apprehensive about his health, and because he had suffered greatly in the last six years due to damages from over-medication. And two of his relatives had died while far away from home, and their bodies had to be shipped back to the United States. I remember when we were on the Queen of Bermuda we were sitting with the captain one night and got a surprise when the captain told us that he always travels with two or three empty coffins, as people can and usually die on ocean cruises. Well, not to be morbid, I told Dad to have faith, and his was a firm positive determination. He wanted to do this Far East trip just for me.

In the month of June 1992 there were frantic telephone calls back and forth to our friends in Japan. We were told not to go to Tokyo, as the hotels were overbooked, and there was no need to go to Tokyo anyway. While Dad had stayed with the Kobarashi family in their beautiful millionaire mansion in Jingumae-do, they actually lived in Tsubame, and used the Tokyo house just for visits. And he didn't want them coming all that way, just to see us. And his other friend, Dr. Yamane, a horticulturist, was now deceased. He had written two books, with Dad's help, about the life of his daughter, Toshio Yamane, who was the first Japanese woman in diplomatic service, (she was killed in a plane crash thirty years ago). The books produced scholarships for Japanese women to come to the United States to study English. Miss Yoshimori, whom Dad knew from her scholarship, had taught the Emperor's grandchildren.

Dad's other good Japanese friends lived southward, and it was agreed that we'd finally stay at the plush Takazono Hotel in Ashiya City near Osaka. We left New York on July 20th, on a Northwest direct flight to Osaka. It was seventeen long hours, and Dad held up very well. At the airport in Osaka was our faithful friend, Dr. Kawachi (who had survived the A-Bomb in Hiroshima). It was evening and once we got settled in our comfortable hotel room, (wearing traditional Japanese kimono), Dr. Kawachi began telling us the plans he had made for our visit. Ogawa-san, who operated the gold-needle factory for acupuncture, popped in for a short visit. He had lived at our Queens house. Another friend at Sanyo had insisted we come down to Himeji to stay with his family the first night, but Dad knew that would be too much traveling, especially since he and Mori-san were liable to be sitting up talking all night. So, it was agreed that Mori-san would come up to Osaka the next morn, to meet us, and to take us by train to Kyoto.

The Kyoto trip was mainly for me, to see all the ancient shrines. I really enjoyed it, and meeting Mori-san's son who was a student in Kyoto. The town was full of students. Everywhere! Dad said it was more crowded than he had seen before. On his last visit he had stayed at the Miyako hotel. He hadn't been in Japan in 15 years and was amazed by the population growth. Everywhere, people, and a little saucy, now that they had more money. Mainly, Japan has a lot of old people, people who remember the war. Unlike Germany, I did not see any evidence of war, but I did not go down to places like Hiroshima. Kawachi-san took us to his beautiful million-dollar home in Ashiya City, to meet his wife, and we had a delightful time playing music and eating good Japanese food. For the final night Kawachi-san took us up in the mountains near Kobe where we enjoyed being in an ancient mineral spa. As was the custom, Dad and I went out in the streets late at night wearing merely our kimonos and gaitas. In such a resort town only the rich people could do it, we were told by our host.

Next, we took Japan Airlines to Bangkok. There, Khun Sanit's son, Pu, met us, with his lovely girlfriend, Anchala. They both went to school in Ohio and were just home for a vacation. So we all could speak English, but Dad got a chance again to talk German as Anchala's mother was German, and we visited her family's palatial compound. Khun Sanit, with whom we were staying, had just been on television so he was wearing his handsome white army uniform. He had been Dad's friend and business partner for more than twenty years. They had met when he was a young graduate student in the United States. Now he was the head of his government's insurance department. And , as a good businessman, he and his wife lived well. Their mansion was right near the king's palace. Soon after arriving they whisked us off to Pataya Beach where they have their vacation home, a place full of marble. Later we visited a farm the family owns, and I was allowed to feed the carp fish which were everywhere in the waters near a temple. But nobody could kill them.

They were sacred. Khun Sanit owned two real old moored wooden ships, and we ate a nice duck lunch on one of them. However, Thai people do eat a lot and we stopped again on our way back to Bangkok, to eat fish out on a shimmering pier where the black waters sparkled from the table lights. And they urged me to try the hot dragon-fly sauce! In that Thai countryside I got to use the native toilet where you apply a garden hose to your bottom. It wasn't as bad as the squatting over a hole you experience in a Japanese *benjo*.

Next back in Bangkok, we did some shopping (suits, shoes, jewelry) and we drove out of town to visit a Buddha shrine park, and Dad had a tear in his eyes because the planning of this he had worked on with Khun Cham Kanchanagom many years earlier, as part of a UN project. And on that visit I got a chance to ride an elephant! That was one reason Dad wanted me to come to Bangkok. When I climbed up on this huge grey animal, I wasn't afraid. Later he ate sugar cane out of my hand. Dad was sorry that he didn't get to visit at the home of his other good friend, Khun Wanchai, of the Prime Minister's office, who was just about ready to retire from DTEC and government service. As a token of their twenty-five years' friendship, and of my father's having worked for the Thai Government for more than a dozen years during his service with United Nations, Khun Wanchai arranged a formal government dinner for us. Other old friends came, even Miss Pissmai Khanobdee who was a fond friend of Dad's, now working with Shell Oil Company. I certainly was planning to tell my schoolmates about all this splendor and reception, the fancy dishes, the gold chopsticks we ate with, but alas, I didn't know if my schooling that September would be anything nice , i.e., where I could talk about my life. High school had been rather bad at times, because our lives were not allowed to shine. But I didn't know then, in just a few weeks college life for me would begin with negative teachers giving me an experience much worse than high school. My lifestyle would be my downfall, with my LD status. Surely not my experiences in life!

On the way home we stopped in San Francisco to spend a few days with our old friend, Dr. Ruth Howard. This time, after a day or so, Dad became quite ill. He had gotten swollen ankles on the plane. His circulation was off; and after having two glasses of wine, he was very sick. But he pulled himself up with care; we made the rounds and had a nice time with our friends. At the end of our stay,

100

we had dinner with her son, Drew, and his wife, who had just adopted two nice blond kids. Still toddlers.

We got home in August and I had to start thinking about my schooling. We immediately got ourselves signing all the papers waiting for us from the college. And I had to take measles shots and get other medical papers up to them. Dad had to find his Army discharge and also had to send them copies of his income tax papers, but all this was merely a waste of time as I would not be getting any financial aid. Next we had to touch base with whomever of the teaching and counseling staff was on campus in the summer. We saw Mr. Paisley and had nice meetings with him, so I was confident that come September, I'd have a nice beginning of my college days at Westchester Community College , but (as I've told you in the Introduction to this book) my expectations were out of line. It became a terrible place for me, merely because of the misguided behavior of an LD administrator and some racist teachers. Dad says you can find such people anywhere, but usually life is good because we manage to avoid them.

Maybe after all this reading you have forgotten what I told you in the Intro and Chapter 2 about my experience with ostracism, racial   injustice,   bold and naked prejudice at Westchester Community College.   Just to refresh your memory: the LD office controls our lives; we have to go through them for everything. The LD woman was out-of-sight until mid-terms when she met with me and my father and put the death sentence on me, saying, I can't read and I can't write (which is all a bold-faced lie!). Further, she wanted me to spend ten years there for a two-year degree. Her office recommended I take an 'easy' course, called College Success, then they gave me F in it.

I remember how pleased the class was with my first paper on an interview three of us made with black Professor Ron Brown. He liked me, and my writing of our meeting with him in his library office was good - NOTHING OF FAILURE QUALITY - yet, in the end a pliable teacher allowed herself to give me F, taking away an A, after influencing from the LD woman who was painting me black with everybody. This college success woman allowed her imagination of my unworthiness to grow; she lied in saying my father wrote my paper. And my other good work for her was my report on the film Malcolm X. You know how few whites bothered to see that film, but believe me, it was very good. And my classmates came and told me how much they enjoyed my report. (There was no justification for giving me F on this. None.) This ganging up to keep me and my father in our place was an act of negative collusion.

Dad is an honest man, interested in my growth. Rather than write my papers, he'd coach me through several writings; I'd improve and come up to satisfactory! No teacher helped me that way! At the same time I wrote on my interview of Prof. Brown, a Croatian student, Sonny, living in our Flushing house, interviewed Dad. Sonny goes to St. John's. He got an A on his paper! I got F!

Students and parents should not have to suffer the death blow of an F without concrete proof. We must have the right to see each and every element that went into that grading, test papers, etc., plus a look at what was given every other student in class. Schools should not allow Fs to be given out in this clandestine manner. Any F grade must be explained in detail. That's the only way to stop this ugly racism.

At WCC, of my two basic skills teachers, the writing teacher had been friendly and half-way on my side. He folded out when his supervisor made herself controlling my future. When a head woman encourages staff to low-grade (F or repeat) an LD student it is not likely she is considering the future of that student. That acting department head wrote a terrible letter to my father three days before the end of the term; ninety percent of it was nonsense from my file. *She had never met me!* And when Dad asked for proof of failure they came up with ten minutes of my test work, leaving out hours of good work. The dean gave us no help; never wanted to see me or my dad in his office. And in his letter to us he said: speak to his secretary if we wanted anything! Only the WCC President Hankin showed any courtesy or warmth. But the scam remained: those acts of racism went unchallenged, and the robbery of my good name. We asked merely for an apology and return of tuition money, but got neither. The matter was reported to the Justice Department. And in January 1993 I transferred to Queensboro Community College, in Bayside.

Also at the start of this book I gave you my like experience at Queensboro Community College. The similarity of failure is striking, and would suggest to a bureaucrat: *of course, this proves he didn't belong in college!* I say, ladies and gentlemen, it's no proof. To me it merely means some well-paid college people, the wrong people, with racial thirst, have been allowed to have a holiday with me, completely forgetting the purpose of their careers. It's absolute baloney that I did not do well. I have several rooms of my papers, and regardless of what they say, I remain an academic person. The plan to x me out was a powerful plan of prejudice. It's the same as the ethnic-cleansing in Bosnia. They knew it could work, and they took joy in doing evil.

Contrarily, I tell you: I do belong in college. My evidence is: I can read and write. I am mature and competent. I can play music quite well; I know rhythm, chords, keys , and some theory. Of course, I don't know everything, and neither do they! And my piano is progressing well above failure level! Yes, with my blind eye, my muscle problem, my body scar, my very good mind, I 'll shout to you this injustice done me! And it happened because (a) I am Learning Disabled, (b) I am Puerto Rican, (c) I've been through the ropes of foster care (which they consider a lowly path), and (d) I now am with a black man, in a single parent home (which they also consider lowly), and , finally (e) it baffles them that this black man is rich! And educated!! This is all I can say about myself, my life experiences, my school experiences, which at the college level have been shock-awakening. In these institutions so well paid for by public taxes, all these unAmerican shenanigans against me, while they gave and give wonderful support to half-competent foreign students in our midst. And these same foreigners, in turn, become nasty to us Americans who have been marked and abused by the system.

At QCC, the spring weather had turned steamy and warm when final exam time came around. Whereas I no longer had my four tutors, Dad and I worked daily to prepare me for my exams. As they were just in review material, reading and writing, plus music, I felt I should have no problems at all with my finals. They were supposed to give me extra time if needed but, ladies and gentlemen, the F grades had nothing to do with extra time. I was counted out before the tests began! And, what did I get for attending their stupid concert, paying big money to hear an average orchestra and soloist? Yes, Dad and I had said it was excellent earlier in this report, but what I'm demonstrating here is that mankind is fickle, and all his capriciousness is in the teaching/listening game. **(Most classmates did not attend the concert and got passing grades.)** I really think there should be a profession called Judging Those Who Judge, or, the Malady of Grading.

My day of tests was May 25,1993. I came bathed, neatly-dressed, and well-prepared academically. I took my tests calmly, thinking I had done all right. Mainly, I knew I was **just as good as** the other students. Going home, I lived through the silent days not worrying about anything. Then when June 2 came and I had to go back to QCC to register for summer school, I got the shock of my life! In that registration room, when we went to the computer to find out my grades, there was a line of four or five, mostly Chinese. The Chinese boys got their grades and threw the little piece of paper on the floor. What the computer-man wrote on me was unbelievable: _A fiery explosion racked my brain!_ They had given me F in one music course, F in the other music course; R (for repeat) in both basic skills classes. I had **nothing** else. Nothing passing!!!

Mainly, I was completely upset that the two music teachers had decided to do this deep cutting-me-to-the-bone. Their idea was to take me down, completely to the bottom. An F!! I wondered how many other students they had done this to. Teachers had such power, but why me? **Music was my life!** I had worried about that piano teacher from the very beginning of the semester and I told Dad I thought he was racist. Dad told me to stick it out, that with just five students in class, he couldn't flunk us all. I was as good as the old-man white student. And if it were a matter of race, I would not be the slowest of the several black kids in the class. But, as it developed, I would not be judged of piano proficiency exclusively. I am certain they conspired to hold me back in view of my father's position in music. They with their music posts and titles could control what happens in music to a black intellectual's son in this horrible way.

By all means, what was in the picture was that spite against Dad, for what he had been able to accomplish for himself in music, and what he was wishing for me. In the end, that spite and their power ruled. They academically had killed me. Of course, we did not know these two so-called music professors. Certainly some could judge them as being of high qualities. But why this mischief against me? If they were really the best people, they could never do this to someone, not to someone normal, not to someone LD, not to someone of color. To Nobody!! All I know, what they've done to me was like murder. Two undeserved Fs, now of public record. . . to scar me forever, to indicate my unworthiness, **and this I will not accept.**

Immediately tears came into my eyes, and Dad patted my shoulder, telling me not to worry. He reached down and picked up several little pieces of paper the Chinese boys had thrown away. When he saw all the As, he knew that the teaching setup at QCC was full of runaway corruption. Their minds were terribly marred, if they could make so much distinction between the work of newly-arriving foreign students and the likes of me, so beautifully exposed at home and in American schools. It had to be racism. And Dad agreed; he was ready to fight with me all the way to Capitol Hill. The pain could never be erased but he would try to get me something honorable, something of what was due me. This had been cold naked injustice. And to look at it in a simple way: America has all kind of laws so people cannot take big money from you and give you nothing. Now, that law has to be applied to the teaching game!

The main thing, he warned me :we pioneers and fighters for justice have to be ready for lies and further abuse. Yes, we had to be very strong people. The institutions support and reinforce even their reeking bad eggs. That brings more critical fantasies, more misjudgment. Was I willing to trudge along that hard path to justice? Meekly I said 'yes'.

Earlier when Dad was advising me not to use the word Jewish in my book, he invited me to come back and talk about it at the end. Well, I came to him one day in late June after reading three hours in my manuscript. We had just had a neighbor pushing us very hard about three little branches our tree-surgeon by mistake cut off his tree. He wasn't interested in the tree-surgeon's name or that he had insurance. He wanted **us** to squirm. He wanted damages from us! Having seen Dad suffer from this, I really didn't want to bother him, but he said, quietly, that he'd tell me a story. He said 35 years ago when he was helping Dr. Boris Schwartz at Queens College improve the symphony orchestra they were just starting, suddenly there was a lot of talk in the newspapers about Queens College being staffed predominantly by Jews. He said he only glanced at the stories and continued working closely with those college professors he knew who happened to be Jewish and also good musicians. They didn't even discuss the issue. But from the publicity, in years to come, he did notice changes in the staff. Queens College became less Jewish and more an example of the American community. Perhaps the same has not happened at WCC or QCC, but he reminded me that always

105

my best teachers were Jews. He asked me to pass it off as a coincidence that I had experienced this present extreme discourtesy and downgrading. I then asked him why particularly were they so hateful to me? He then reminded me that some persecuted people who were new in America, or new in decent jobs, they might, in a controlling position over me, deal too harshly. Theirs was a *learning problem*, not necessarily racial. It was sad that they did not see a need to be friendly. Perhaps they were blinded by an ideal, a fear or just plain ignorance, or even envy. In spite of their power over me, I should remember **within myself**, I am in no sense a failure. I'm active still and can work myself away from the pain and price of such prejudgment, knowing <u>I am someone</u>, regardless of the tattoos they've tried to put on me.

For a minute, I felt better. Dad wanted me to accept the fact that broader matters than race control our lives. And where someone has failed me, I was to turn the other cheek. ***No! It was Racism!***

Quietly he said the issue was more than race; it was poor supervision and administration. When professors can get away with such, something is amiss in the education system as a whole! Now I spoke of poor Mr. Rosenbaum, killed in Brooklyn, and asked why the people did not equally remember poor young Cato, first killed. Dad had no answer. We agreed we'd work on the broader issues, so our discussion moved back to academic institutions. He said they had a duty to steer their teachers away from such bias and bottom-grading. ***All teachers must love the student more***, have empathy, Jews and nonJews. None can really make you a failure in subjects you love. Still, I have a duty to fight any bad markings, remembering my basic power is: I **can** read; I **can** think; I **can** play music.

Dad smiled, saying we could have a piano brought into the courtroom, to show the judge I can play, and he would restore my life. But what if the judge is Jewish? I asked, and if he said I didn't do *some particular* piano lessons well? Dad laughed , saying a good judge is merciful and would realize the system needs more checks and balances. He told me to forget   jewishness, and   finally reminded me that a black woman had been among my worse teachers. Yes, and mainly I should remember good teachers, Jews included. But, I told him in the end, if I had gone to a Catholic college, or a black one, this F-wipeout would ***never*** have happened to me. Never! He smiled, saying public institutions still have some good people. I was too wounded and too young to agree entirely.

In June 1993 Dad took me to London again. He had planned to see his good friend, George Leopardi, of Australia, but we missed them by three weeks. This time we were going to the Queen's birthday celebration (she had about five thousand invited guests and about a thousand of us who were not invited). During our 1990 visit my dad's good friend, Mr. John Saunders, who had held many senior positions at UN Headquarters and was also the UN Representative in Lebanon when the war was at a crucial point in that country, took us to dinner at the Royal Overseas Club in St. James, but this time he was ill and we would not see him. Nevertheless, like other good people, he was busy at work with a biographer doing a book on the late Sir Robert Jackson, whom we also knew. We brought my friend, Jason, along on this trip to see Queen Elizabeth II. I also took him alone to Madame Tussaud's, the Tower of London, and the Dungeons.

Our hotel in Earl's Court was quite a ways from Leicester Square, the kind of Rock area where Jason and I hung out. We did go with Dad on a visit to Hampton Court, Wimbledon, Windsor Castle, and to a friend's Erif Rison, whose eighty-year-old mother, Maia, came up from the south and enjoyed seeing Dad after thirty years. Erif's brother Mark was at Cambridge, and her father, Stuart, was a high UN official in Geneva. I'm telling you this because our friends naturally asked me about my schooling, and I had to tell them a bit of my sad story. They couldn't believe it. How could I be a complete washout with my talents, my spirits and with having seen so much of the world? And, I had gotten around this huge Londontown quite well. Yes, Jason and I could go most any place in town by ourselves. Are we mentally defectives with limited ability in schools? People who can't make it in education? I asked Dad if I could stay in London and go to school there. He first wanted me to prove I was American by fighting the bad people who had denied me my education at home. Yes, if my energy held up, and I could later come to London with no fear of not doing well. Nobody there told me I didn't belong there, or, that I couldn't make it in any of their schools. I'm sure their school teachers would treat me <u>with respect</u>. I liked the British. They seemed like very nice <u>cultured people;</u> none of that rabid racism I had come to know like an expert, <u>in my home, America.</u>

***** ***** *****

CHAPTER TEN

In December 1992 when I first got the report from WCC that I'd gotten all failing grades, I became very depressed because I knew much of my work had been good work, worthy of a C grade. I didn't know then that I'd be going to QCC next, or, that I'd get the same treatment there. I thought my WCC experience was the end of the world. I had no more chances in college, and no chance for a job. I sat home completely depressed, and it was Christmas time. I guess a school never thinks about us when they send out such wicked mail. Now I was no longer a free individual. After all that trouble and time they took to get us in, all that signing of papers, taking physical exams, all of it, to let us go without even a decent good-bye. Well, it's clear, the minute they decide you're no good, they are through with you. They've got your money. They don't care about your feelings or about what happens to you. Teachers and administrators participate in this negativism without any guilt.

I was troubled deeply. In fact, some days I was sick. I felt much like the Homeless. After a few days, the shock of it subsided. I still liked to read books so I went daily to the library. I really was desperately lonely in the library. I happened to see on a table Rachel Carson's book "Silent Spring". My father had recommended this to me but I never got around to reading it. It's about ecology and all the birds and animals in nature dying from pollution caused by man's excessive waste, and his use of DDT. I thought: I now have a death watch on me, caused by people with excessive greed, who would take my share and say I don't deserve an education. It's frightening not to know where your future lies.

And I had nightmares. One night I woke up screaming: Kalkut was chasing me with an ugly spear, and behind her with knives was Reznick, Silverman, Putnam, Pieters, all those who had been evil to me at WCC. Suddenly a knife flashed and blood began to flow from my arm. I yelled out "Mercy" and they yelled back: "We told you, you didn't belong here! We told you!" I woke up in a sweat and decided to get out of the house. To the library again. My refuge.

So in my library visits, like a homeless man, I sat pondering what we are, and why some of us should control the others. I remembered all the time Dad had had to spend, gathering papers, getting what the college wanted at my admission, including my having to sign up for the Army. All the hopeless details, then they drop you like a wooden spoon. Without explanation! I didn't have to leave WCC but my father got me out of there in time. He knew that the LD woman would continue pestering , and I would get nothing.

When in June my demise at QCC became certain, this was even harsher. I got two Fs in subjects I certainly knew, then swiftly a letter came saying I was on **probation**. Hah! Like a prisoner! <u>And once again, no letter ever explaining the F grades.</u> F grades in subjects I knew so well! **This is Wrong!** One hundred percent wrong! Dad with his 55 years' experience in music wrote right away to QCC President K. Schlemmer, but he received no reply. Not in these several months waiting while the book has been in its final stages. Yet, they were so quick, **rushing a letter of probation** to me!

Again I had my nightmares. This time about the two music teachers, Rosenblum and Cannalakis, who did me in. I was playing piano for them. They stood by just laughing at me. Laughing at my playing, at my scars. The piano teacher shouted, again making small of my disability (even though he himself was disabled), telling me nothing was wrong with my hands when he wanted me to play certain fingering. Soon the other one came up, sticking his viola bow down my throat, and the piano one, in his wheelchair, rared back and kept laughing at me. After a moment's blackout, I saw knives again. I put my hand to my chest and the sticky red blood made me gasp. I heard yelling:"This is for Crown Heights! This is for Crown Heights!" I knew nothing about Crown Heights. I told Dad this after I quickly woke up in a cold sweat. He smiled, telling me it was only a dream, that I was reading too many mystery books. From the furrow in his brow, I knew he was worried for me, very worried for my future. Actually, I was equally worried about him. I knew in his poor health, they could kill him with such injustice to me. And if he died, nobody would care. I'd be alone in the world, with no education, and no chance at an education.

Well, I heard psychologist M. Scott Peck tell Oprah: all life is a schoolroom. We have to take time to watch a snowflake. That's quiet time. My life has been War because of the cruel stealing from me. Some call it Backlash, which means America's Civil War still is not over. So in idle time, I will look at the beauty of a snowflake, as I rearm to get my life together.

***** ***** *****

Now, ladies and gentlemen, I want to give you a bit of my brain which I worked out while sitting so lonesomely in the library: a list of suggestions what the government (including school districts and colleges) need to do to improve what's out there for us, the Learning Disabled. Here is my whole list. See what you think of it.

I.   Eliminate grading. Once a child is admitted, let him concentrate on getting finished. When you give exams, make sure that he passes. If he doesn't pass, give him a new teacher. The teacher is more or less the problem when a student doesn't learn.

2.   For the Learning Disabled, always keep the parents in the picture. Give them equal say-so with the teacher. Make the parents join a committee, and attend regular sessions (at the high school or college). They are there to participate in their child's education. . .to assure that he gets an education.

3.   No failing of students without a shred of evidence. All test papers must be given back to the students. If parents and students do not agree with test results, they should have the liberty of having another kind of test (oral, multiple choice), and of going higher for review and redress. Teachers should be made more responsible; there should be no 'secrets' of test papers. Teachers should be responsible that students pass. When students fail, some of the teacher's salary should be taken away. This way, they would be less apt to use the failure grade. Two or more tests should be given in the semester, i.e., perhaps once a month. This will eliminate all this trauma about failing as a result of one or two (unseen) tests.

4.   Other than grading by class work, add credit for work or life experience. Teachers for LD students must always think about job-relatedness in grading, not cold, academic grading. Learning Disabled people are always anxious about their first job, whether or not they'll be accepted, and can do the job. Work experience needs crediting at both high school or college level. And, be a little considerate of LD status, EFFORT must rate much higher than it

does for normal students. And, credit PROGRESS. And as for life experience, I certainly should have received some transcript credit for all the world traveling I've done. Individual teachers do judge us miserly, and as near-idiots, making us stand still, and, no one teacher's grading prejudice should rule our lives. Always **a panel** should be involved in grading LD students, giving due credit for effort as a part of performance.

5.   Students must be given a chance to grade teachers, if grading is kept. Getting through the course must be equally shared by student and teacher. Right now, the teacher is the policeman and jailer, the student is the slave. And don't let them continue to grade us by *what's in our files* (our prior records, our handicaps).

6.   Be practical in judging a person's shortcomings. In my own case, they'd make much of my small stumbling in reading, forgetting completely that I have a little speech defect, and I only have vision in one eye. And allowance should be made for the fact that I was crippled in language comprehension by passing out of infancy without a clear mother tongue. Further, teachers are not there to judge my foster care experiences, downward, as they do. Finally, I have my long, hopeless nevi scar that makes me a bit shy in talking aloud. Don't expect me to talk up exactly like normal children, and don't grade me down for my slightly less command. Do not grade LD students DOWNWARD because of their various shortcomings.

7.   No negative decisions on LD students without EQUAL participation of student and their parents. In my own case after giving me failing grades they said I didn't go to a practice lab or two when nobody had told me during the term the lab was compulsory. If parents and students met regularly with teaching staff, with equal voice, useless remedial work could be streamlined.   Too few LD specialists and teachers realize how little time the LD student has with all the extras they put on him. No, these extra sessions must be agreed with the parent!

8.   So-called LD professionals have too much power, too much say-so in the decisions related to the student's future, his life! To minimize this flaw of prejudgment, the student and his parents

111

should have *equal voice*, and never should the LD specialist be allowed to a) design a lowly plan, b) keep the student repeating, and, c) influence the student's teachers! The whole idea of having the professional is to **help** the student upward! She is not to judge him downward. She is not a physical doctor; she knows little of his abilities or his life. Her silly reading of his file is not to limit his future!

9.   Don't go at failures in an assembly-line fashion. Give the student a break after his first failures, and by this I don't mean that hopeless letter-writing telling one he has failed or that he is on probation. Be gentle with failure (if grades are kept). None of you is God and you shouldn't act as though you were! Listen to the student and find out what is wrong. A panel is a better listener than a half-evil teacher. Don't put all the blame on the student.

10.   Do not throw students out of college without due process. In the review, the student's side must be heard. **If test papers have not been shared, the teacher must be punished.** Let the student give a written account defending himself, to be judged by an impartial body including his parents, and not the teachers who have failed him. He should be given freely a second chance.   With sympathetic teachers and a different set of circumstances, he might very well achieve, admirably.

11.   Due emphasis must be placed on SELF ESTEEM. Teachers and LD specialists must say positive things to LD students, not rip them negatively all the time. Rigid negative viewpoints on the part of teachers and staff as to the worthiness of a student to go forward must be discouraged. The student's efforts are paramount. If he is there every day, never a failure! Every student's reputation is his life. Any general review of failure should include full airing of the student's complaints against the teacher and the institution, and the panel should be willing to reverse the decision if the student can make a good case for himself. No negative transcripts should be written on LD students. They have a rough enough time without that extra burden.

12.   Equally, emphasis must be placed broadly on **intellect** and not specifically on day-to-day demonstrations of academic achievement. In my own case, I knew Spanish orally quite well, but I

was thrown out of the class just because I was a bit slower than the average student in picking up verb endings. In time, I would have mastered the grammar quite well. Just think, if I lived in a Spanish-speaking country, I as an LD student would certainly know my own language. So, an American wanting to learn Spanish, certainly could, if the teacher had a little PATIENCE.

13.   The main emphasis must be put on **passing** students, and not failing them. If a teacher wants to fail a student, she should be brought before a panel to argue her case, and the child should hear it, and give his views. The student's successful completion must be the goal, not this throwing him out which is so prevalent, so **barbaric.** At college level, when they suggest **withdrawing** an LD student, it's a scam, to keep tuition money and student earns nothing. Avoid it; fight it!
Again, if the teacher is allowed to flunk a student, she should pay a fine. Every time.

14.   No independent actions should be allowed in down-grading of LD students. With panel reviewing, the idea needs sharing with somebody important to the student, *before* any failure grade is given. The LD student needs more **compassion**, but he seldom gets it. Just as the president of a college, or principal of a high school, signs the almighty diploma, *they too should sign each and every failure slip sent out on an LD student.* Why? Because it is equally an important and grave matter.

15.   Preparation is a judgmental word. Over-proud teachers love to twist the screw in expecting so much of LD students. Let them learn to think of **time**, and of themselves as being more delinquent than the student.   In my case, they never explained things; I always had to get the explanation at home. Too often the judgment of an LD child is that he must learn things more quickly, and perform equally, with the normal child who has had more time and more explanation in his classroom. Be flexible and think timewise when you judge the work of an LD student.

16.   Teachers need to think: CONCENTRATION ON CAREER. Nobody   should have to sweat through a first year in college with so much added remedial work and re-judging your past

113

when you already have a high school diploma equal to that of any other student! So, get out of your mind all those negative criticisms you want to pile on that person. Get on with teaching; there should be no threat of failure! You're paid to educate; teach LDs pride, **pride in accomplishment.** Think positive; <u>BE HELPFUL</u>, not killing. Teach **hope.** Ready for a career! Most importantly, suggestions of repeating should be discouraged. *You won't make the LD student perfect by having him repeat.* His time is important too. And, you, teacher, you are not perfect!

17.   Americans (even in the teaching profession) must realize they are very racial. Three-fourths of the failures among Blacks and Hispanics are not due to ability, effort or performance, but to negative teachers putting down their racial hate. To discourage this, Afro-American and Spanish kids must have an extra share of grievance redress, as they must face prejudice and negativism worse than any other student. When you study the percentage of them who graduate, realize the many who don't make it because of naked racism hiding in the institution's closets. **Denigration** is very much the practice in American schools.

18.   Equally, negative tabs have been put on learning disabled students. *Stop judging them by their files*, and as first of all 'mentally-deficient'. Teachers need to realize how stupid they've been: because someone needs a bit more than so-called normal students doesn't mean they're idiots! It's not a sin to be needing, or, a bit slower than others! Administrations must **watch** what teachers do to LD students, and sway them away from concepts that we are less brainy than the others. We may be slower, but not less brainy. Teachers have always treated me as if I were nearly a moron, and this writing lets you know I am not that low a person. The country doesn't need such inaccuracy , such cruelty, among teachers.

19.   LD students could make it in regular classes, if **watchdogs** were there. Teachers **do** take out their frustrations on us, and grade us down. Nobody cares about **my innocence.** And, I can't be guilty of low grades <u>without proof or trial</u>. **It's unAmerican!** With this flaw in colleges, we cannot equally achieve and finish. I also recommend *student panels* to review campus procedures and advise

broadly on text materials, teacher performance, and mostly on this idea of grading, this deciding WHO IS WORTHY. If schools can tolerate poor-performing athletics, for the sake of the team, they can also tolerate poor-performing LD students, for the sake of America. Since it is quite likely that they, the institutions, will continue to take our money and treat us like dirt, I therefore recommend:

20.   For the Learning Disabled, _separate colleges_ must be established so that they need not compete with normal students (like the special school for the deaf, Gallaudet College in Washington, D.C.) This is a great need mainly because of teacher impatience with us, and the constant grading down of LD students. Since we know that we can achieve in any field, our own institutions would help us to do it with more self esteem, and with greater numbers of our people being successful. As you know, we are mostly steered away from the white-collar world. They want us in blue-collar stuff. With our own college, we could study what we please, and there would never be this prejudice talk of: We can't Read, We can't Write, We Don't Belong There!!

21.   Finally, there should be established nationally something called Educational Crimes, and judges will sit and decide in all cases where students are failed and pushed out. While he is to primarily judge the teacher and the institution, he can also judge the student and decide if he is serious in his efforts to get an education. If the student is serious, that should be paramount, and not the quality of his mind (with poor people judging this). And, _teachers should be fined_ and even put in jail for spoiling a student's chances, giving poor grades without justification, because, really, they are killing that human being, killing his future.

*****   *****   *****

CHAPTER ELEVEN

Well, I'm now in my third college within one year. Disgraceful? Perhaps, but not to me. I regard it as, still, my golden opportunity. And one cannot lecture to make me think I was a poor student in the first two, one who could do better. No, the onus was not on me but on other stigmatizing, arrogant and race-crazy people. **I did my absolute best the first time, and the second time.** It was possible for me to have this third chance in that initially I had been accepted at six schools. I did not bring with me my ugly baggage of the two rotten transcripts showing me as a completely worthless student. That really isn't me, and my new teachers know it. I was so relieved that Dad found me this wonderful place, where I can be somebody again. It's a small college with no airs. They don't believe in grades. They are accredited. We get private tutorial instruction. And, they'll certainly guide me towards my degree, *and that's all people go to college for. Why should any teacher take my money and give me F?* An editorial in the New York Post on July 1, 1993 mentioned racism at CUNY (New York's colleges). It talked of a policy started 20 years ago guaranteeing **"a spot somewhere in the system for every high-school graduate"**. It mentions Susan Sontag and Dr. Leonard Jeffries, but it does not talk of *getting rid of* so many racist teachers who give us Fs!

I now know what a prisoner feels like when he gets sentenced, does his time, then comes out hopeful for a job. Mine has been an invisible prison, but like James Brown and Mike Tyson, I've suffered most from very harsh judges; a payment lined with hatred. Father Montalto of Good Shepherd Church in the Bronx tells me you can turn a negative into a positive. And, people with compassion have to believe in you! Father Montalto says he grew up in a mixed neighborhood, and that everybody loved each other, and, the first he heard of racial discord was when he went to Central High School.

116

WHY in higher schools do people get airish about who they are? Why must they live and practice that kind of superiority?

Back in my early school days at P.S. 55 in Queens, I had a mean teacher called Miss Silver. Once I wrote her what I considered a nice story; it was about ghosts and haunted houses. Well, she took it and tore it into little shreds right in front of me and the class. I think I turned red, even with my Spanish complexion. Last week I gave my new English teacher a story about my recent visit to England and to spooky Hampton Court, where King Henry VIII lived. People working there had told me the palace was haunted, and I wrote my story on this. I actually felt cold breezes as I walked around those huge and ancient drawing rooms. Guess what, ***my new teacher liked it! No criticizing, no Fs.*** In fact he said I had written a very fine report. It made me so happy to have ***at last*** proper appraisal of my work. And, I would have been equally happy if he had given me a B or a C. But no Fs. I am not that lowly. Guess again, my new piano teacher says **my playing is good.** No Fs from her! All those who graded me as lowly, I feel sorry for them. I am the same me that Miss Silver wrote up as 'hopeless material' years ago. And, ladies and gentlemen, it is so nice to have the approval of educated people whom you can trust, teaching people who will approve you! People with compassion. I know Dad would not have rested in his grave with me as a total failure in college. No, he is not dead yet, but all those negative WCC and QCC college teaching people, trying to steal my future, almost killed him as they went about trying to kill me. Well, we're both in safe territory now. We're among rational good people.

My dear mother, in her hospital bed for more than a decade now, and my dear grandmother, home with a broken hip (from a lady in the Bronx pushing her on a bus), both have been so encouraging to me as I seek to become an educated person and not a street person. How can I tell them how badly I was treated at WCC and QCC, robbed and left without a fighting chance? Going by a file, labeling and subjecting me to ridicule: ***proposing only a possibility of failure.*** I want to have a job. When Dad passes I want to take Mom out of the hospital, bring her home. Support her. **I can do it, if you let me get prepared!** I remember Gloria Steinem in her Self Esteem Workshop with Oprah Winfrey. She said children only believe they're important when they're treated as if they're important.

117

I've heard one of the last good deeds President Bush did was to sign a new Americans with Disabilities Act. I have not read it yet, but I'm glad if it can help us. But like a racing car or train that kills people, it may be too late to save me. I was always isolated in schoolrooms, not enough friends, not enough cohorts. I'm ready now to join groups as I realize this is how we gain strength for neglected causes. The neglect of LD kids needs early correcting. When they waste our lives in schools, it will only cost the government more, if and when we go wrong. Inside I'm still the bookish, half-prepared artistic child I was that first day in kindergarden. But I'm more bitter now. And I should hate all those very proud (superior-thinking) teachers who tried to kill me. Like Father Montalto says, I'll let compassion work on me. I can still play my music, write my poems. Bad teachers can't take these things from me, but I still need that diploma to get a job, evidence of time well-spent.

In the evening of July 12, 1993, we received a phone call from a canvasser for *B'nai B'rith* (thinking we're Jewish by our name). He spoke of anti-Semitism on college campuses, and wanted a donation to help 'get' people like___(he named two black leaders). Well, I know now like Dad says, the Jews are excellent organizers. Afro-Americans also need this! And Learning Disabled need it! Freedom to seek redress should not be neglected.

On Martin Luther King Day, January 1993, I heard President Clinton say Americans have to be prepared to make sacrifices. Teachers with too much power (me saying) should give some of it back; we slow students need more power. And the President said he didn't like that Who's-up and Who's-down business, that it "doesn't amount to a hill of beans!" (Same as grade-categorizing in the schools - me saying!) Then I heard Mrs. Clinton say that Hope is not just a town in Arkansas, it's a condition of the human heart, something that binds us together. Yes, they've reminded me: I am a person with **potential** who thinks we need binding together. Those greedy ones will have to give up something. And, I cannot let those negative people in education rule or ruin my life.

During my darkest days, in December 1992, I heard on television about a New Jersey Santa Claus, in proper red and white uniform, telling a little Afro-American boy: "You wanna see a monkey? Look in a mirror!" My WCC and QCC people, in proper uniform, thought I was a monkey. In that same December 1992, the most wonderful thing that could ever happen to an LD student happened to me. Just as WCC gave me a Christmas present of F grades, (feces from their toilets) , I got a beautiful personal note from President-elect Clinton. A letter had told him my problems; straightaway, he took the time to send me in his own handwriting such a beautiful encouraging note. He signed it not "Professor", not "Sir-Almighty", but simply "Bill". Here, this very important man, leader of America, this real Santa Claus, taking time to write to me so humbly. So warm! Yes, and it made me cry again. These were happy tears. And from that letter, I got courage to go on with my life. Dad wrote to him, thanking him. By that time he had become really President, and the handwritten personal notes could come no longer.

In that same time Dad heard from Ambassador Stephen Wang in Chile, inviting us down, and from Tong-liang Hsieh in Taipei. Most busy with correspondence,he'd written Dr. Johnetta Cole, president of Spelman College, whom President Clinton had heading his transitional team in Education. (Dad is establishing a scholarship program at Spelman, the school of his mother.) People in the Afro-American community , if they are old enough, know that Spelman was a showcase school from post- Civil War days. Like Howard, Fisk, Talladega, Lincoln, Spelman drew girls from the best Negro homes one hundred years ago. Mrs. Laura Spelman (Rockefellers' grandmother) was instrumental in starting Spelman, and Dad's grandmother , Lucinda Hutchins, worked with her to get the proper atmosphere and cadre of dignified young ladies wanting education and a solid life, in times when many Americans thought Negroes did not have such fine culture or upbringing.

As for the Spanish part of his family, the Rodriguez part came with the adoption of a son by Mary McLeod Bethune (who founded Bethune-Cookman College in Florida, and was a great friend of Eleanor Roosevelt). That son married Dad's Aunt Margaret whom I met at Riverside Church in New York. She in her seventies is still fair and beautiful. I've also met her son, Edward Rodriguez, who lives in Europe. But my real purpose in telling this is to let you know that I am now in a family as American as apple pie. For more than a century they've made themselves responsible Americans , not particularly thinking color or race. But there are evil ones who will grab onto us (like they've grabbed on to me) and denigrate our preparatory road and our contributions. And from my position, there is no way that I could be in such a family without an education, no

119

matter how my white teachers _delight_ in twisting my roots and saying I have limited capabilities. While Dad has known princes and countesses, he thinks upward in life is **simple** living. Thinking how teachers want to floor me, he spoke of the Kennedy family years ago having had an unbalanced girl who unfortunately had to be put away. But I'm neither a Kennedy and I'm not unbalanced! I don't want **teaching people** putting me away! And I'm not thinking grandly of myself in this comparison. **Teachers,** all I want is **my due:** a simple chance to be myself and to be respectable. Merely, **YOU** have to stop exaggerating, and see me as a deserving _upward_ being!

Many LD students could make it, if treated honestly. And it should not irritate teachers if some of us darker LDs do come from high culture families where education is important. And such families are not going to let them exaggerate with their profiles and bad thoughts about us, grading me so that I cannot make it. The Learning Disabled world, I'll say one final time, needs pushing up and not pushing down. While many of us come from better roots than our teachers can imagine, we need an education and the route to it should not be an imagining game! If they would just DO THEIR JOB of teaching us rather than trying to drag us down, the world would be a better place. (These words are from the Dickens book I read four years ago.) Yet, I'm not supposed to know reading or writing, _REMEMBER?_

I recently saw on television a story about a school system in La Verne, California (I think it was El Camino School under Dr. Mary Higgins) where they decided to use boys in prison to help out with handicapped children. Now, just imagine in some areas people might think these boys were doing harm to their children. Well, it made the prisoners happy to be useful, and the poor handicapped kids were joyful to have every day somebody especially interested in them! Also I saw on television where Mr. Art Chambers in Johnson City, New York has learning disabled in the same class with other kids, including severely handicapped kids. Lesson plans are modified for each child. Support services for this don't cost any more, and the benefits are better because the children are treated as if they are important. It was said: _They are making Progress, and that's what education is about._

I learn a lot from television. Last week I saw a program on the building of the national cathedral in Washington. I thought: college too is a great temple, like a cathedral. What is it for? With tracery windows, like jewels, to flood our world with light. To dazzle and inspire. . . **where God touches earth**. Then I remembered, Dad had four cathedral windows put in when he remodeled the house for me. And my gargoyles! Yes, I love my home; it is my cathedral. To keep it I merely need to earn a simple living, but there are those who don't even want to see me get this much security. This chance to sustain what I already have. No, they want to _push me down_ to some low stupid profile where they think I belong.

In most areas, we still have this terrible malady of teachers not believing Learning Disabled or Handicapped kids have the right, the need, the aptitude or the where-with-all to get a full education, or even a passing grade or degree. They slay us with imperfect testing procedures, then stay blind to our spotted mastery. And you know: _The testing procedures are not God!_ Teachers, if you keep this eagerness to fail, then America's education system will continue to fail. I do not have to fit your exaggerated profiles of who I am, nor your barometer of how much I have to achieve to merit your biased okay. Yet, I shall keep fighting for honest appraisal and _**full credit**_ for my hard work at school, to the reaching of my full goal and potential, my life. Whether or not I am an adopted minority kid , originally from the ghetto, it's nobody's business but mine. I should have _my full opportunity_ at education, instead of this categorizing, this downgrading, you've pulled off.

Now, for the real mystery of my life and this book: I've had **never a day of trouble** under my private tutors. I've excelled with them. Yet, there is a different story with teachers in the public institutions, and paid so well by them. By now you should be able to solve this striking mystery of A over here and F over there. So, please, do something about it!

Dad thinks it's a mistake what they're teaching Afro-American children today, this over-emphasis of _roots._ He says Melville Herskovits established sixty years ago that most Afro-Americans (72%) have mixed heritage, and if the Japanese can embrace western civilization to get ahead, certainly the teaching of Blacks should return to it, as they are Americans first. As for myself, I am glad I've managed to muster enough energy to resist the racism and prejudice of my so-called professors, and other such negative teachers in high school and grade school. And I am glad too to have had the precious time (just a few minutes) of such a magnificent leader as President Bill Clinton.

As I'm not qualified for any job, my striving is not over. If I have to do it without teachers' help, I can. Dad says I've been so dutiful to my schoolwork, I've lost a lot of youth, that sitting around with friends, going on picnics, or just watching the sun rise. (He's been most upset hearing me say *"I can't"* once that WCC LD woman entered my life. And I've had to fight to get rid of that stigma of a loser she's put on me.) Normalcy became doubly hard for me to regain once those dishonest academic people began pushing me down, stealing away my goodness. I can stay youthful and feel happy with myself if society won't let them rob me **any more** of my chances for full development, and *my* academic degree. In our efforts to get the discrimination at WCC and QCC reviewed, the New York office of the U.S. Dept.of Education treated us not good (as if they'd forgotten their mission). We've kept Washington informed, and still expect the Justice Dept. to act in the end. Dad believes like the White House that somebody really needs to reinvent government! As for me, I believe there should be some friendly, untangled road to redress for me, as I was beaten and innocent in this F-grading done to me.

Through President Clinton I now have a revitalized spirit to keep trying academically. I do want those people in Washington to remember that we Learning Disabled are free Americans too. We should have voice over our futures; we should have purposeful passage. And in our own privacy we can pray for the President as he tackles the tremendous task of Rebuilding our Education System. We know he will reclaim control, and that will help us in our struggle. Our spirits are hopeful. And, ladies and gentlemen, I didn't even get HOPE from those teachers who were so proud of themselves as they went on, like butchers, WASTING MY LIFE!

***** ***** *****

THE END

122

(top) Dad in his UN Work, circa 1975

*(l.) With Miss Charles, Pres.
       UN Travel Club,
       in Antigua. 1987.*

(r.) Dad relaxing at home, 1987

SOME POEMS

by *JAMES MIRANDA*

*(top)Khun Wanchai and
his family, Bangkok, Thailand
< Me and Khun Sanit,
on his boat*

With Dr. and Mrs. Kawachi, in Japan

SOME POEMS
by James Miranda

***** ***** *****

FREEDOM

I am a Child of God,
filled with peace and goodwill.
There is strength in my mind,
And skill in my hand,
And with spirit I sing Aloud.

If you will not allow me passage,
There are other golden roads,
Yet, I can always walk free
Among the Clouds.

The Goal of Faith

I am Listening, Holy Spirit,
for your guiding word.
I don't have to be perfect;
I know I'm not a Nerd.
Will I know you thru flowers, or sunlight bright?
Bless me with ideas, that speak of your Might.

All the bad happenings,
You'll surely redeem.
Don't be too hard on
those who scheme.
Put them far from their sin;
Let them serve, O Father, in our club,
that of loving men.

San Turce, Puerto Rico

Judy and I, in Dusseldorf, Germany

Me at Baden Powell's house in London

Peter and I, at Battery Park, NY

The Jakob Family visiting us in New York

WAR STORY

People should learn what life is about,
  because one day war will break out.
  And they'll all be running to save
  their necks,
  When all through the years
  They never cared heck.
  On that great day freedom troops arrived,
  To help you eat and stay alive,
  Yes, they were black troops,
    like raspberries,
  They made Buchenwald free.
  And how you forget it
  Worries Me!

THE LD MORSEL

America, a land of plenty, you name me
  LD student, always with Eees.
  You don't leave me cheese or air to breathe,
  Yet your books teach of a democracy
  with everybody acting peachy nice,
  But I know with you, I'll always be mice,
    paying your tricky price.
  You want me to learn this fully plump democracy
  While marking me down for all I can't be.
  My appetite must settle for your meager pea.

Yours is a nice smile for the Oriental running free,
  to keep on your worthiness ball.
  For us , a sneer, as you grab your weekly fee,
    while letting us surely fall.
  Your rulebook says we must stay in a stall;
    We LDs know that sassy gall.
  Ours is a dark endless path,
    while you look for flaws in our math.
  No crumbs are left as you bite with full joy.
  We're only labels, an LD toy.
  We'll tell the world this pit of wrath,
  Where you've denied us with your greedy ploy.

PROFESSOR WHO CAN

Who can study and get better
all the time;
Who can get on a big stage
and offer a good rhyme;
Who can play a lovely tune,
and not even expect a dime?
For the talent God gave you,
you'll share this favor;
You'll teach it to a degree.
But 'long comes a Black
paying you his fee;
and your poetic music gift
begins to show a drift.
You give him F for
Lord Knows Why!
You've killed yourself
in your wicked try.
So, who can you be -
A musician great?
You, my friend?
You're only a Fake!

ON BRAVERY

They flunked me out of school,
with lies
So that I would have no future,
no ties.
These mean evil people you must
call professionals,
But as humans they're
quite exceptional.
Theirs is a power game,
And I'm always one plucked minority
to blame.

Oh, how they love searching my
past,
Looking for a pea, an ant or flies,
Something in that spy glass,
to criticize.
Maybe on one page a footnote
says how I did not cry when my father died.
They don't see it as an asset.
"All worthy children must fit our facet:
Father, mother, color, brother,
That's the only way to discover:
I'll mark you down,
You worthless clown!"

I went thru twelve years of this folly.
Now I hear voices in my sickman's garrett:
"You were brave, by Golly!"
But hospitals don't listen to
A brave molly or wally,
Nor to any caged Parrot.
"Besides, your record clearly says:
You're not Molly or Wally;
You're a babbling polly!"

ANNEX I

Dear JJ,

From our exhilarating visit to London last month, I still hear the beautiful Sunday calling of the morning bells bursting forth around St.Paul's. I saw the delight in your face as we walked from Blackfriar's to church. Then, again, I saw your eyes sparkle, and your deep breathing of joy when the great old organ before us growled out familiar hymns we both knew, which you had heard on our organ at home, and in my servicing as AGO organist in the great churches of Westchester. Yes, much in London was familiar in your life. The world is a small place, and you know the years and centuries don't mean much. Yes, quite likely you've been there, and here, before. But I know first in your mind is all that vulgar shouting you've experienced at home in America: YOU DON'T BELONG HERE! That from so-called college teachers. Well, last evening back in my own bed, I took joy in reading the last chapter of your book; it brought tears to my eyes. It's full of marvelous sensitivity , all that charm that made you a Londoner four hundred years old. I feel blessed having had the good fortune of sharing life with such a wonderful son who knows the world and will give it something when he leaves its shores.

When I first met you seven years ago , there was a tingle of magic working , and we discovered we shared the same July birthdays. In all our visits around the world, you took in knowledge, to share it, and it's alive again in "Wasting My Life". As you know, God always comes to us in a cool refreshing breeze, or in a ray of sunshine beaming down. I am satisfied after reading your good work that He has blessed you with many unsung talents, just as He has blessed me, and every man merely wants a son to join him in discovering the world, mastering a few things, and sharing the blessing. You have done this, winding up a useful servant of the world. In spite of all the wickedness you have endured from biased, half-American white teachers who thirst to shine out as superior to you. Don't worry about them! You are safe in God's hands. Their damaging you won't take away the talents, rare to the world of men, He's given you. Of course, you know your religiosity impressed me on our first meeting, as well as your forgiving smile. And the seven years we've shared has been bloody battles, staving off the charlatans trying to steal your goodness, actively trying to destroy you because of your few (I say 'few') disabilities. Your forgiving nature means you have been listening faithfully to the Holy Spirit. You know your tasks are not easy, and I am proud of you for sticking with them. And for your growing knowledge and understanding of your fellowman, weak as he may be, and forgiving him for his evils toward you. All this makes you a shining example to the world. And you've been all these good things while they keep shouting that you are inferior.

You'll remember the 16th century German fortune-teller and magician, Faust, who came among people to bring joy to the world. While street people liked his magic and the idea of his supernatural gifts, he also had disbelievers, and they made it so hard for him that he became disillusioned by these critics. So he made a pact with the devil, Mephistopheles, to give him increased powers for 24 years, after which time he agreed that his soul then belonged to the devil. Well, you know there were several versions of his story among French, German and English people. You saw the Christopher Marlowe version in England; you saw the Goethe notes at the museum in Düsseldorf; and I reminded you when we visited the Köln cathedral that that was where Faust was supposed to have found religion in 1532. As time passes, the story of his life gets changed, and we still do not know if he were mainly a good man or bad man. Well, your life has been much the same - with evil teachers biting at you, weakening you, while I try to build you up to keep remembering you are a good person capable of great knowledge. God has put you into the world to serve, not to be gobbled up by wicked teachers who won't give you a chance.

While it is not easy to forget and forgive those who maligned you at WCC and QCC, you must, and go on with your life. You are alive and God has plenty of work for you. You liked Dickens' "ATale of Two Cities", and I was very proud when you finished reading it.You understood better those trying to push you down. And you can tell Mrs. Edelman you will survive, that your Father has put the seed there that biased teachers can't kill. JJ, I'm proud that you've remained strong through all those disappointing storms. You have learned from life and that is more than any over-proud professor can teach you.Your life will always be just as useful as theirs, as the sacred essence of life they could not steal from you. After so many months of college, working hard, you have no credits, but as the hero in your Dickens' book said: 'There is a better life'. Now you too have a book, and through it, hopefully, a better life, some hope, some new opportunities, and likely the meeting of new friends. Eventually you'll have a chance for a job, and to continue work on your academic degree (which should not be denied you).

When they didn't understand your disability, it was, always, you lied, you didn't do the homework. They attacked your honesty, your integrity. This means they were ill-trained and ill-supervised. And they've harmed you. No, you don't have to meet the world on their terms. Yes, this has been an outrage. Yes, they are terribly over-paid when they wreck people's lives like this. Are we going to do something about it? Yes, indeed; I'm with you! Mainly, those who tried to destroy you did not know the Fellowship side of life. How they loved to say you could not read or write when reading and writing has always been the food of your being! Moreover, these two are the unfinished need among all men! So, how can you, James, particularly you, be perfect at it? Mainly, they don't want you to have the credentials! Plain and simple.They've robbed you, and left you naked, but your life will go on. . a very useful life.

Kind of lay aside the label `Learning Disabled'. You have the full human component, as much as any man. Moreover, you have the joy of mental strength, which helps you build physical strength. And you have the joy of faith, and through it, hope. Those horrible black-and-white exaggerations, in fancy college buildings, cannot destroy you. Remember, our greatest gift, our greatest strength is that of good deeds, and they can't take that from you. While they certainly criticized your deeds as not good enough, the world has other judges. And you'll remember: your deeds are your sword that will give you power throughout life. You have not lost your battle. The world is on your side. And keep that spark of creation, like Edison and Ben Franklin, you have something to give. You'll help bring forth a new age of brotherhood, away from sham, hypocrisy and stealing. I believe the world will absorb your goodness, not theirs. JJ, I'm proud to have you as my son. You're not going to let the wolves eat you up! You have fish and bread to give to the world. And, thank you for joining me and enriching my humble life.

Love,

Dad

131

ANNEX II

Dear Reader,
On behalf of my son, James, I thank you for taking an interest in JJ's book. I hope you have enjoyed it. When he first asked to do it I had my doubts, then soon I realized it was the only thing at that moment in his life. He had unjustly been given failure grades when his achievements were steady and very good. As James has adequately explained, there were several reasons for this lynching. Americans with job power (including teachers) often abuse it terribly. Most of all you should know that while carrying this heavy burden , James remained dedicated to his school efforts. At home, I allowed the house to get a little messy, because in all the schools they were demanding too much order and perfection from him. And in the end, they gave him absolutely nothing for his money, time and efforts. In the seven years he has made commendable steady progress, and I am proud of him. The slashing of James at college was brutal and unforgivable. Nobody is that important, as they tried to be, or, should I say 'superior'. Yes, it was a game of making him 'inferior'. The unreasonable poor grades came as a sudden blow, as lethal as if someone were hit with pneumonia. I had to drop everything of my life to save him. It was a twenty-four-hour-a-day struggle. Slowly the self esteem is getting back to normal. True to his nature, he has remained cheerful and hopeful. He is graciously ready to forgive those who have damaged him so. As soon as I spotted his plea for help, I understood it, and pitched in, responding as best I could. Basically I knew he was honest and devoted, and that I must fight to save him from such lechers.
I helped James get started by reviewing eight years of my personal diaries, giving him those matters chronologically of which he was a part. Many crude incidents had to be left out, but it was a joy for both of us to relive the happy moments with friends in so many different places in the world.
I certainly remain a champion for all Learning Disabled students, knowing how they have been harmed by teachers and administrators. They need all the help we can give them (and, they are remarkably able to carry on, if given half the chance). There is nothing more that I can add to JJ's wonderful story, "Wasting My Life".

Yours sincerely, his father,

R. Crowder

132

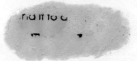

N.N.